BORN IN 1943

HOW TIMES HAVE

CHANGED

ELIZABETH ABSALOM & MALCOLM WATSON

D'AZUR PUBLISHING

Born In 1943
How Times Have Changed

Published by D'Azur Publishing 2023
D'Azur Publishing is a Division of D'Azur Limited

First published in Great Britain in 2023 by D'Azur Limited
Contact: info@d-azur.com Visit www.d-azur.com
ISBN 9798367909463

ACKNOWLEDGEMENTS
The publisher wishes to acknowledge the following people and sources:

British Newspaper Archive; The Times Archive; Front Cover Malcolm Watson; p4 United States Library of Congress's Prints and Photographs division; p4 Derby Telegraph Bygones; p4 Forces War Records; p7 sallyantiques.co.uk; p7 Wartime Information Board, CC0, via Wikimedia Commons; p15 Historic Royal Palaces; p15 Constable50806; p17 Wisdom learning; p19 a-e-g.org.uk; p21 Bill Brand; p21 www.ianvisits.co.uk; p25 21stCenturyGreenstuff : p25 U.S. National Archives and Records Administration; p27 ruslanguage; p29 Ministry of Information; p40 Fashion History; p41 Etsy; p41 Quora; p42 Johan Persson;p42 The Enid Blyton Society; p43 Abe Books; p44 PiccoloNamek: p44 Malcolm Watson: P47 londoncouncils.gov.uk; P48 Richard Cannon; P49 www.planet-sputnik.com/english-rose-kitchen-blog; FineArtAmerica; P54 blue17.co.uk; P55 Prisma Watches; P56 The estate of John Hopkins, Bill Brant; P57 Butlins; P60 Malcolm Watson; P64 Alexandre Prévot, DeFacto - Own work, p66 Victor Hugo King; p65 NASA; p64 eBay; p65 Quatro Valvole; p86 MacDonalds; p894 Vintage Dancer; p100 Science Museum; p100 JodyKingzett; p101 NASA; P101 Salvatore Barbera; p105 Eduard Marmet airliners.net; p106 Wadhurst History Society; p120 Atreyu own work; p120 David Merrett; p123 YouTube; p125 Cédric Janodet; p125 Ken Fielding; p131 Juan Solis; p134 Ethical Trekkin; p134 davidoffnorthide; p151 Corporate Finance Institute; p153 Kingkongphoto; p138 This file is licensed under the Creative Commons Attribution 2.5 Generic license; p146 Dave Comeau; p146 John Douglas

Whilst we have made every effort to contact copyright holders, should we have made any omission, please contact us so that we can make the appropriate acknowledgement.

CONTENTS

LIFE IN

Monarch: King George VI   Prime Minister: Sir Winston Churchill – Conservative

In 1943, Winston Churchill's inspiring and resolute leadership was guiding the country through yet another year of rationing and austerity, virtually every household item was either in short supply and had to be queued for or was unobtainable. The blackout continued to cause widespread inconvenience; unnecessary travel was regarded as anti-social; Lord Woolton made a famous 'pie' and we were all asked to eat more potatoes and less bread.

News was of paramount importance and promulgated through the newspapers, the cinema and the radio. Half the nation would tune in to the nine o'clock news each evening.

But there was also a greater sense of optimism that the war was being won – and planning was beginning for the future. In 1943 the first of over 1.5 million American servicemen arrived on British shores to prepare for the Allied offensives and there was a feeling that after victory, the country could not go back to pre-war social conditions.

Queuing for bread (above).
US Forces arrive (below).

FAMOUS PEOPLE WHO WERE BORN IN 1943

6th Jan: Terry Venables, Footballer & Manager
29th Jan: Tony Blackburn, DJ
25th Feb: George Harrison, Singer & Guitarist
9th Mar: Bobby Fischer, American Chess Player
5th May: Michael Palin, Comedian & Presenter
27th May: Cilla Black, Singer
17th June: Barry Manilow, Singer Songwriter
26th July: Mick Jagger, Rock Singer
18th Dec: Keith Richards, Rock Guitarist

FAMOUS PEOPLE WHO DIED IN 1943

7th Jan: Sir Henry Maybury, Civil Engineer
28th Mar: Sergei Rachmaninoff, Soviet Composer
3rd Apr: Conrad Veidt, German actor
30th Apr: Beatrice Webb, Socialist & Reformer
27th May: Arthur Mee, Topographer & Author
1st June: Leslie Howard, Actor
22nd Nov: Lorenzo Hart, American Composer
15th Dec: Fats Waller, American Jazz Pianist
22nd Dec: Beatrix Potter, English Author

1943

Born in 1943, you were one of 48.25 million people living in Britain and your life expectancy *then* was about 63 years. You were one of the 16.1 births per 1,000 population and you had a 3.1% (the lowest rate yet recorded) chance of dying as an infant, most likely from an infectious disease such as polio, diphtheria, tetanus, whooping cough, measles, mumps or rubella.

The country was living under unprecedented regulations governing every aspect of life, no-one in your family would be 'untouched' by the war and you would be reliant on rationing and ration books for some years to come. But, you were at the beginning of the end of the war, the country was planning for the future and the future was to turn the old 'social order' upside down.

Paper was severely rationed and 'The Times' and 'Daily Mirror' both ran to only 8 pages. News was often delayed for reporting – for example, details of storm damage or new machinery - to prevent information 'helping' the enemy.

In 1943, the standard rate of income tax was in excess of 40%, a higher rate was charged on incomes over £2,000 and saving was encouraged. The country needed money to fight the war. Clothes were rationed but when not 'making do and mend', the government had intervened in the mass manufacture of high street fashions with the arrival of the purchase tax free, 'utility' clothing scheme. Accommodation in cities was often scarce, unscrupulous landlords raised rents, and agricultural workers were provided with Government cottages. Cheap 'utility' furniture was made; central heating was unheard of, coal fires heated houses – and coal was rationed. When you heard the air raid siren you might go to the Anderson shelter in the garden; children helped with the harvest; cinemas thrived for entertainment and newsreels and by 1943 more than 1,300 pubs had closed due to enemy action but 'the local' was still a comforting place to go to - and everybody seemed to smoke!

WAR TIME BASIC RATIONS

On *average*, one adult weekly ration:
Bacon and ham – 4oz (110gms)
1s 10d (9p) worth of meat – about 8oz
2oz (50gms) butter
2oz cheese
4oz margarine
3 pts of milk
8oz (230gms) of sugar
2oz tea leaves
1 Egg

JANUARY 1943

IN THE NEWS

WEEK 1   **"New Year Pageant"** Representatives of all the armed services attended the Royal Albert Hall. Flags of the 'Empire and Her Allies' were paraded and held high as the auditorium stood and sang 'Abide with Me'.

"Health is Better Despite War" The Minister of Health confirmed that, in the fourth year of the war, our nation's health is better than in peacetime.

WEEK 2   **"Ministry to Find 'Knockers-Up'"** An unofficial strike was called off after the Ministry of Labour promised to supply eight men from the Labour Exchange, to act as knockers-up for those workers on early shifts at the LMS Railway at Nottingham.

"National Service Acts Extended" Women who are between the age of 19, lowered from 20, and 31 will be called up for industry.

WEEK 3   **"Army to Eat More Potatoes"** It is the *'idle nibbling of bread'* that the Minister of Food wants to stop and see more potatoes eaten instead. The Army is to substitute 3oz of potatoes for 1oz of bread and 4oz for 1oz of flour.

WEEK 4   **"Babies Given Away Like Railway Parcels"** The Council for the Unmarried Mother and her Child are concerned about the number of adoptions of unwanted babies being arranged without proper safeguards.

"Black Market Threat to Toys" As The Board of Trade has prohibited toys retailing at more than 26s 6d (£1.32) after March 1, parents are being warned of the likelihood of black marketeers cornering the expensive toy market before next Christmas.

HERE IN BRITAIN
"Women Sort the Letters"

Specially trained women of the ATS are taking over an increasing share of the work of the Army Post Office which deals exclusively with all forms of mail for the Army and the RAF overseas. There are about 2,500,000 letters a week, including about 100,000 6d air letters.

The sorters' duties require a high degree of intelligence and skill as owing to the large number of different arms of the service in the British Army, and the sub-division into regiments, battalions, batteries and so on, the sorting is by no means simple. The auxiliaries each deal with about 8,000 letters a day.

AROUND THE WORLD
"Absent on New Year's Day"

Over a hundred ringleaders, in advance of hundreds more men, were charged in Sydney with taking the day off on January 1st without 'reasonable cause' and in contravention of the National Security Regulations which had made December 28th a holiday instead.

There had been no official union protests when the rules changed three months ago, but more recently, some workers protested that they were entitled to the holiday on December 28th in lieu of Boxing Day which fell on a Saturday – and therefore they should be paid extra rates on New Year's Day. When this demand was refused the men took the day off anyway.

Before the war 218,000 tons of bones and 27,000 tons of fat were imported into Britain each year. This has now ceased and all bones and fats, which are wanted more than ever, must be collected in this country and the Army is a major source. A hundred tons of bones can be made to produce 12½ tons of grease, from which five tons of nitro-glycerine can be made, sufficient for the explosive charge of 40,000 18-pounder shells. That same 100 tons of bones can be turned into 12 tons of glue and 50 tons of fertiliser or pig food. The average amount of 'swill' per man in the British Army is 4lb a day and all fats and bones are collected.

The heavier side of the salvage work is just as efficient. Officers in charge carry a magnet in their pockets to identify any metals they find, and they love all old papers, books, letters, rags, cardboard boxes, bits of rubber, anything washed up by the sea, broken-down lorries, cars, bicycles, old prams, toys or clothes. One officer collected 100,000 used petrol tins, borrowed a steam roller to flatten the mountain and sold them on.

Unfortunately, the average soldier needs convincing of the value of this 'rubbish', so a mobile exhibition has been made showing the various forms of salvage and its value. On just one table in this exhibition is a 32-page copy of The Times from July 1937 and alongside it, a table covered with things that can be made from its pulp, including bowls and the inside part of a crash helmet. Many a dispatch rider dashes round Britain, Libya, Syria, or elsewhere, with 'the leaders, the letters, the court page, the law report, city prices and the births, deaths, and marriages' round his head.

FEBRUARY 1943

IN THE NEWS

WEEK 1

"Chorus Girls Oppose Sunday Theatre" Representatives said that the profession did a lot of work on Sundays and raised an enormous amount of money for charities. If there were commercial opening, they could not do that.

"Rare Fruits for Bomb Victim Children" Lord Louis Mountbatten brought a bunch of rare bananas from Casablanca for Princesses Elizabeth and Margaret, but the girls asked to give them instead to children injured after their school in Lewisham was bombed.

WEEK 2

"Anti-Dim Wipers for Gasmasks" Special impregnated cloths to prevent condensation on the eye panels of civilian gas masks are to be issued to the public. There will be no charge for the cloths which will be packed in small tin boxes.

WEEK 3

"Young Wives Must Have Children" A population 'expert' from Oxford has warned that unless young mothers agree to have no less than four children now, Britain will dwindle to a '*small and unimportant State*' within 50 years.

"The King's Sword for Russia" King George has ordered a sword of honour to be offered for presentation to the Warrior City of Stalingrad, to show the admiration felt by himself and the peoples of the British Empire.

WEEK 4

"Fewer Ladders in Rayon Stockings" The Board of Trade has introduced new specifications which will improve the wearing quality of stockings and an extra allocation of cotton yarn will ensure the heels and toes are strengthened.

"Newspapers for Services" Welfare organisations are requesting that once read, instead of immediate salvage, newspapers are 'passed on' to men and women in the Services who, because of their hours of duty, are unable to obtain any of the limited supplies.

HERE IN BRITAIN

"No Orchids for Miss Blandish"

The GPO no longer allows you to send flowers through the post. The first blow to the flower sending Romeos came when the Government banned acceptance of all flowers and plants by rail and then, last year, it became forbidden to send flowers or plants by parcel post. But there was still the letter post left, and the GPO agreed to allow them to be sent in this way.

But the concession has been so abused that now the ban is to be made absolute. And so, if 'Miss Blandish' still insists on orchids you will have to take them along yourself.

AROUND THE WORLD

"What's In a Name?"

A baby boy born in Brooklyn, New York, has been named Adolf Hitler Mittel. The child's father is of German Austrian descent and incidentally sports an unmistakable Hitlerian moustache. "*I cannot see anything wrong in naming my son after Adolf Hitler*" he said, "*After all, lots of children are named after persons in the same category such as Napoleon and Julius Caesar.*" 'G men' are expected to visit the Mittel's home to inquire why an unemployed woodcutter sees fit to rank the world's most hated ex-house painter among the world's greatest men.

FOOD FOR OUR TROOPS

Army rations are sufficient, if there is no waste, to supply troops with four good meals a day -breakfast, mid-day, tea and supper - but meals are not good unless they are well cooked and served hot. Army chefs and instructors all attend the Army Catering Corps Training Centre at Aldershot where the equipment is equal to that of the best hotels. Before the outbreak of war, expert caterers were placed in key positions as advisers to the Army, and when war began, their number was increased by the granting of emergency reserve commissions to caterers with the requisite qualifications. About 40,000 men have already taken the Aldershot courses and by the end of the war, the three services together will probably have trained as many as 100,000 cooks.

However, field service conditions bear no resemblance to those of an ideal training centre. Army cooks must know a good deal besides cooking with the latest appliances, and Aldershot is not training cooks for the catering industry - although many thousands will be competent to take good places in the industry after the war - but for the army in barracks, in camps and on the field of war where the cook will often have to improvise. Training is done in the open-air as well as in the kitchen and here the students learn to use portable camp equipment such as Bluff and Triplex ranges and Soyer stoves, improvised oil-drum ovens and the primitive kettle trench. The Army also uses hay and insulator boxes in which food brought to cooking heat over a fire will finish cooking in a moving lorry while the unit is on the march. The Army Catering Corps is a combatant corps and in appreciation of the services of its cooks, the Army awards them extra pay.

MARCH 1943

IN THE NEWS

WEEK 1   **"Wings for Victory Objectives"** London will lead the whole country in the savings campaign next week with a target of £150,000,000. Preliminary events heralding this gigantic effort begin today.

"London Shelter Disaster" About 178 people were killed and 60 injured when the crowd entering a London tube shelter after the alert, tripped up and fell on top of one another, blocking a stairway. There were nearly 2,000 in the shelter.

WEEK 2   **"New National Loaf"** People have been eating a new national loaf containing home-grown barley, and in some districts, oats and rye as well. There have been no complaints and apart from the bakers, the public does not seem to have noticed.

WEEK 3   **"More Milk for All"** The liquid milk ration is to be increased by half a pint to 2½ pints a week. The mild winter has helped supplies, but rather than raise allowances further, stocks of preserved milk must be built up over the summer for the forces.

"Paid Adoptions to End" Childless wives who try to evade call-up by adopting a baby will be stopped. The Home Office is to bring back into full operation the Provisions of the Adoption of Children Act postponed at the outbreak of War.

WEEK 4   **"Access to Coastal Areas Restricted"** Restrictions on travel will be in force to a depth of 10 miles inland along the East and South coasts from the Humber to Penzance.

"Home Grown Meals" Two out of three meals eaten in Britain are now home-produced saving on shipping and imports. For every 100 tons of food produced before the war, we now produce about 170 tons.

HERE IN BRITAIN

"X Ray Pioneer"

Peace as well as war produces heroes. Harold Suggars, who has died from X-ray dermatitis at the age of 65, was the last of a gallant band of four X-ray pioneers in the London Hospital's X-ray department. The healing value of the rays was discovered in 1896 and Suggars, a former carpenter, volunteered to become assistant to Ernest Harnack, the X-ray expert. They showed him Harnack's hands, already deeply scarred with X-ray dermatitis but he was not deterred. He knew the dangers, but suffering humanity came first and within twelve months he too noticed the first signs of the agonising, dread disease on his own skin.

AROUND THE WORLD

"140 Years of the Sydney Gazette"

1803 saw the publication of Australia's first newspaper, the 'Sydney Gazette and New South Wales Advertiser'. As well as shipping news, town gossip and commercial news, the paper reported on government proclamations, regulations and detailed court appearances. George Howe, the editor and publisher of the paper had been transported to Australia for life for shoplifting in 1800. With previous experience working on the London Times, he was quickly designated Government Printer, using a small wooden printing press brought out with the First Fleet, in a lean-to shed at the back of Government House.

The task of collecting ordinary domestic materials in the household, belongs to local authorities, and in the first year of the war they collected 774,452 tons, in the second year 1,053,016 tons and in the third year 1,438,538 tons. By the end of 1942 the number of salvage stewards enrolled on a voluntary basis to help in collecting valuable waste material was 130,500 and school children are acting as junior salvage stewards under the guidance of members of the Women's Voluntary Service.

This week the Minister of Supply, spoke of Britain's remarkable achievements in salvage, saying that since the beginning of the war our recovery of waste paper had reached almost 3,000,000 tons; salvage of waste rubber, since the rubber scrap campaign was started last March, had considerably exceeded expectations and kitchen waste was being recovered at the rate of over 2,000 tons a day. In total, about 820,000 tons of domestic scrap has been collected during the war but the salvage of paper was still disappointing.

Nine months ago, an order was issued making it an offence to throw away or mix paper with other materials, and for quite a time, litter virtually disappeared from the streets and the countryside. But lately, careless disposal of paper has become a serious problem. However, housewives were complimented on their salvage of household scrap. Enough is collected each day to provide sufficient feeding stuff for 210,000 pigs, but a great deal is still lost because many people think that little bits are not enough to matter. From one economical home a few scraps might seem a trifle, but from millions of homes it becomes a considerable contribution, and even now, 50,000 tons of meat bones taken home every year are never heard of again and the equivalent amount must be imported, occupying valuable shipping space.

APRIL 1943

IN THE NEWS

WEEK 1   **"The RAF is 25 Years Old"** To commemorate their twenty-fifth birthday, the King, for the first time, approved the RAF mounting a guard at Buckingham Palace for four days.

"Bicycles for Lonely Troops" The people of Norfolk have given £500 to buy bikes for soldiers on lonely searchlight and gun sites who are unable to enjoy their off-duty hours, being stuck miles from the nearest town or village.

WEEK 2   **"Holidays at Home Again"** To induce Londoners to spend their summer holidays at home, the LCC will provide opera and musical comedy, ballet, circuses, concert parties, band performances, fairs, swimming galas, boxing tournaments and dancing.

"WREN's Anniversary Parade" The fourth anniversary of the revival of the Women's Royal Naval Service was celebrated in London by a ceremonial parade of 1500 Wrens at Horse Guards Parade. The Queen took the salute at a march past at Buckingham Palace.

WEEK 3   **"Women for Home Guard"** Women are to be recruited to the Home Guard in the ratio of 20 to 100 men. Safeguards are set out so that the civil defence services will not be affected by the loss of women recruits.

"Book Salvage" 417,905 books were collected in the national salvage drive in Oxford. Many valuable or rare books were taken by the Bodliean library, but the majority will be pulped, and the rest go to the forces, children's hospitals and war damaged libraries.

WEEK 4   **"No Proxy Weddings"** The Government has said 'no' to men serving overseas being able to marry by proxy. The authorities said the decision *"would leave many innocent babies as illegitimate and cause hardship and sorrow to thousands of decent British girls."*

HERE IN BRITAIN

"Roads for the Future"

A skeleton system of high-speed roads, referred to as 'motorways', is advocated by the Institution of Highway Engineers. The motorways will be reserved for motor traffic only and there should not be access to them except at relatively infrequent intervals. All intersecting roads should be carried over or under them; gradients should be easy; transition curves, both horizontal and vertical, should be used and, on horizontal curves, superelevation for speeds up to 100 miles an hour should be applied; they should have a good non-skid surface and land should be reserved for refreshment rooms.

AROUND THE WORLD

"Black Market Take Over"

Former associates of the gangster Al Capone have almost complete control of the US black market. They have taken over huge packing plants and food distribution warehouses. In Chicago 'Black Market Incorporated' owns seven large meat packing plants. The authorities moved this week to stem the huge flow of black-market meat pouring into New York and New Jersey neighbourhoods. Seven companies were charged with bringing 5,000 tons of this meat into New York between December 16 and January 31 and selling it at £500,000 above regulation prices.

THE ROYAL AIR FORCE

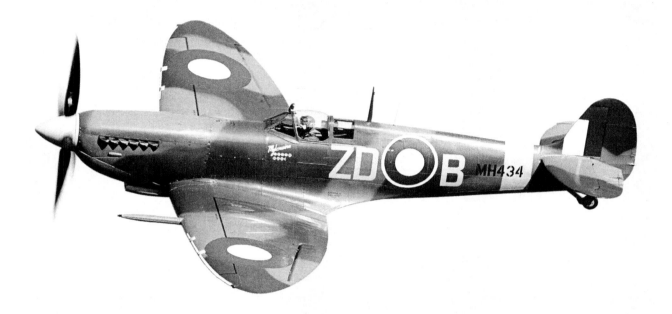

The RAF Spitfire

Mr Churchill has been awarded his honorary wings, the flying badge of the Royal Air Force. The honour was conferred this week on the twenty-fifth anniversary of the formation of the RAF, formed at a critical period of the last war, by the amalgamation of the Army's and Navy's flying wings, the Royal Flying Corps and the Royal Naval Air Service. It came into being after three years and eight months of war and its twenty-fifth birthday falls after three years and seven months of an even greater war.

When the war of 1914 started, the aeroplane was a new and untried weapon, strictly limited in its uses and not sure of its role. Rapidly it developed both as a weapon of offence and defence. When the allies mounted their counter-offensive in 1918, the RAF was able to concentrate 1,290 first-line aircraft against its opponents' 340, and, enjoying this air superiority, was able to disrupt the Germans' communications and harass their troops by low flying attacks. When the Armistice came, the RAF was the greatest air force in the world, both numerically and in quality of equipment, possessing more than 200 squadrons, 22,647 aircraft of all, 103 airships and a total strength of 291,000 officers and men. After the war the Service shrank to a shadow of its former self but managed to keep many members possessing a pioneering spirit, which in turn, maintained the high standards and increased the prestige of British aviation throughout the world.

At the beginning of this war, we had far fewer planes than Germany and the country has undergone a massive drive to build Spitfires and Hurricane fighters, and Wellington, Whitley and Hampden bombers. All technically superior to the German planes, but it was, nonetheless, a dangerous situation until the Battle of Britain had been won.

IN THE NEWS

WEEK 1   **"New Order for Part-Time Workers"** More people, mainly women up to the age of 45 with family responsibilities which do not permit them to take full-time work, will soon be directed into part-time work in industry and business.

"Housekeeping Savings Belong to the Husband" An Oxford County Court Judge deemed that money saved by a wife out of the housekeeping, maybe to buy their clothes or having the occasional hairdo, is legally the property of their husbands.

WEEK 2   **"Pay-As-You-Earn"** A Group of Conservative MPs have given support to the principle of relating the income-tax of both manual and non-manual workers to present rather than the past year's earnings.

"Prime Minister in Washington" Mr Churchill has arrived to renew discussions with President Roosevelt. This is their fifth meeting and carries with it the presage of fate, for each has been followed by momentous events.

WEEK 3   **"Miners Work Extra Day"** Scottish miners have decided to work an extra day to produce an additional 50,000 tons of coal, as a tribute to our armies for their African victories.

WEEK 4   **"Smaller Knives and Forks"** Standard cutlery is to be manufactured in 'rationed' sizes. There will be maximum material-saving lengths for carving knives, forks, bread knives and steels and one size of table knives, tablespoons, dessertspoons and teaspoons.

"One Result of Clothes Rationing" In the two years that clothes rationing has been in operation, it is estimated that 500,000 tons of shipping space normally used for the importation of raw material and finished articles, have been made available for transporting troops and munitions.

HERE IN BRITAIN
"Water Fit for a King"

When the King inspected an Army division in the Eastern Command, he saw Royal Engineers demonstrating how the Army makes itself independent of water supplies by purifying river water and making it fit to drink. Watching the Sappers working their sterilising plant, the King asked to sample the water. He drank from a tankard pure, clear water which only a few minutes before had been taken, brackish and muddy, from the river. *"It is very good,"* the King said, adding with a smile, *"but you had better ring me up tomorrow to make sure that it was all right."*

AROUND THE WORLD
"Debut of the Duke of Alba's Daughter"

The coming-out ball for the Duke of Alba's only child, Donia Maria del Rosario Cayetana, Marquesa de San Vicente del Barco, began just before midnight and lasted till dawn, at the Palace of the Duenas in Seville and was the most brilliant social event since the days of the monarchy. Over 3,000 guests representing many walks of life in Spain were present. The 15th century Mudejar palace provided a perfect setting, with its floodlit Moorish Garden, where people danced to modern music or listened to typical Andalusian folk-music.

CONSTABLE OF THE TOWER

The Constable of the Tower of London and the ceremonial gold key.

The new Constable of the Tower of London was installed this week in a ceremony that reaches back almost 900 years. About 20 Yeoman Warders formed a circle on the grass, dressed in scarlet and gold with tricolour rosettes and ribbons. In the centre stood the Chief Warder and near him the Yeoman Gaoler carried the gleaming processional axe. The Lord Chamberlain came out from the King's House carrying a ceremonial gold key on a red velvet cushion. Behind him walked in procession the new Constable, the Lieutenant of the Tower and the Resident Governor and Major of the Tower. The band struck up a Royal Salute in honour of the King's representative, who had come *'in the King's name and on His Majesty's behalf, to deliver the Keep and Custody of His Majesty's Palace and Fortress of the Tower.'*

The role was established by William the Conqueror around 1078 and the holder was then known as the Keeper of the Tower and historically, he controlled the operation, upkeep and security of the Tower and everyone who lived and worked within it. He was also responsible for the Tower's, often famous, prisoners. In return for his service, the Constable was given the right to seize any swan that swam under London Bridge; any horse, ox, cow, pig or sheep that fell into the Thames from the bridge and any cart that fell into the Tower of London's moat. Every ship that came upstream to the city had to moor at Tower Wharf to unload a portion of its cargo for the Constable and although the role is largely ceremonial today, this tradition is still upheld at the annual Ceremony of the Constable's Dues. When a ship of the Royal Navy visits the Port of London, the Captain presents a barrel of wine, his 'Dues', to the Constable on Tower Green.

IN THE NEWS

WEEK 1   **"Protection Against Diphtheria"** A new campaign to immunise 75% of the total child population of Britain against diphtheria was opened yesterday. In just two years, the Ministry has managed to get half the children of the country protected.

"London Calls for Telephonists" Among the civilian jobs which women do, few are more important than the telephonist. Within the next 12 months the Post Office will require 2,000 more for London alone.

WEEK 2   **"Help for Farmers' Wives"** Domestic work on farmhouses may now, in cases where hours interfere with work on the farm, be an 'approved' category for war work and farmers' wives will be given domestic help.

"Dead Soldiers' Pay" Claims for the return of pay and allowances issued after the death of single servicemen have caused a good deal of bad feeling and anguish for parents.

WEEK 3   **"Scarcity of Shoe Leather"** The Ministry of Supply has stated that the country is facing a period of real shortages for the footwear industry and people should refrain from purchasing shoes they can do without.

"Knights in Armour" All crews of American heavy bombers will soon be going into battle clad in protective armour. 16 lb sleeveless vests of manganese steel, called 'flak waistcoats' have already been proved to be highly successful.

WEEK 4   **"The Stalingrad Sword"** The King has approved the design for this sword of honour. It will be inscribed on one side: *"To the steel hearted citizens of Stalingrad the gift of King George VI, in token of the homage of the British people".*

HERE IN BRITAIN

"Nun Wins Epsom Derby"

A nun has won the Epsom "Derby". Not the real Derby, but a race run in aid of Epsom and Ewell's 'Wings for Victory' week. Mother Veronica who runs a riding school for children, entered the horse 'Saudades' as a million to one chance. He is only a hack and the children's pet but ridden by former real Derby winner, E Smith, the horse beat several thoroughbreds.

There were other famous jockeys in the race too, Gordon Richards included. Mother Veronica was very surprised but said, "Saudades will remain the children's pet, we will never enter him for another race."

AROUND THE WORLD

"Russians Love of Flowers"

Russia is being swept by a craze for flowers and the flower-sellers in the Moscow streets are doing a roaring trade. The convoys of lorries which traverse the capital are decorated with bird-cherry. Generals and children, tram drivers and sentries, all carry flowers.

Part of the Leningrad highway is patrolled by women guards who work with sprigs of lilac tucked in their belts beside their revolver holsters and those off duty have garlands of flowers round their forage caps. They all know that there will again be no country holidays this summer and that the present light heartedness is likely to be short-lived.

In October 1939, the British Ministry of Agriculture launched the 'Dig for Victory' campaign. Food was 'a munition of war' and with shipping space at a premium for the war effort and imports hit hard by the attacks on shipping convoys, in this time of rationing, people across the country were encouraged to grow their own food in their gardens and allotments. Keeping people fed at a time of food shortages and maintaining national morale were key goals for this propaganda campaign, which resulted in the creation of 3.5 million allotments in Britain by 1943.

The severe shortage of imported wheat meant that the Ministry of Food were desperate to have not only the Army, but also the civilian population, eat potatoes instead of bread. The undoubted star of the 'Dig for Victory' campaign was 'Potato Pete'. Along with 'Doctor Carrot', he lent a jovial image to the entire enterprise – and gained something of a cult following, with songs celebrating his efforts becoming popular.

On the commercial side, professional horticulture was equally important and this month, at a meeting of the Farmers' Club, the lack of qualified personnel and first-class research programmes was discussed. The Secretary said in his address, *"Horticulture has never received the acknowledgement to which it is entitled, and even to-day, when much prominence is given to farming activities, little is heard of the horticultural section's contribution to the national effort."* The time is opportune to give serious consideration to obtaining vegetables in greater variety and an increased acreage of those which could be served alone, so that the housewife might have an easier task in furnishing an attractive daily menu. If it is found necessary to make a further reduction in the meat ration the public will be still more dependent on vegetables. A first-class research station for vegetables is needed.

JULY 1943

IN THE NEWS

WEEK 1

"War Factories Cover 3sq Miles" Our new Ordnance factories are so big that some have as many as 700 or 800 separate buildings, with twenty miles of roads, railway stations and lines, and hostels for thousands of workers.

"Glider Crosses the Atlantic" A fully laden glider has been successfully towed across the Atlantic by a transport aircraft for the first time. The 3,500 miles from Montreal was accomplished in a flying time of 28 hours.

WEEK 2

"23,000ft Delayed Drop" A young RAF pilot from New Zealand has made an involuntary parachute descent which is a new world record for a delayed drop. Stunned and partly blinded when his plane went into an uncontrollable spin over the Burma front, he fell 20,000ft with his parachute unopened, more than the 17,000ft previous record.

WEEK 3

"Utility Braces" Men's braces which have been scarce and high priced, will be available in Utility styles. Made of leather and webbing, they will be cheap. Boys' size 1s ¾d (5p) and adults' range 1s 1¼d to 3s 6d (17p).

"Mr Bevin's Warning for Boys" The Minister said that the serious shortage of manpower in the coal industry would mean resorting to some desperate remedies during the coming year. *'I shall have to direct young men to the coal industry.'*

WEEK 4

"Mussolini Resigned" The King of Italy has assumed command of the Italian armed forces and Marshal Badoglio is the new Prime Minister. But the war goes on.

"The Churchills Go to the Zoo" Mr and Mrs Churchill went to London Zoo to see the four lion cubs of which Mr Churchill's lion 'Rota' is the father. The African lion was presented to the Prime Minister in February.

ONLY HERE
"A Paper …"

A correspondent of The Times has written to inquire if the Ministry of Supply ever received the instruction *"to save everybody's time by condensing official papers and avoiding official jargon".* He was driven to ask the question by the receipt this week of a 'Special Direction' made under the Control of Paper (No. 48) Order, 1942, which had come to him from the Deputy Controller of Paper for the Minister of Supply. **Here is the first Paragraph**: *Notwithstanding anything contained in the Control of Paper (No. 48) Order, 1942, Directions Nos. 6 and 7, the Minister of Supply hereby directs in lieu of the provisions thereof that you shall not (subject to the provisions hereinafter contained) …*

IN BRITAIN
"… Consumption Puzzle"

… consume in the period 27th June, 1943, to the 30th October, 1943, in the production of the news-bulletins, magazines or periodicals mentioned in the first column of the schedule to the Special Direction (hereinafter referred-to as the previous Direction) issued under the Control of Paper (No. 48) Order, 1942, tinder Control Reference 166/43, a quantity of paper (including any paper printed or made outside the United Kingdom) the aggregate weight of which exceeds the weight set out opposite that news-bulletin, magazine or periodical in the second column of that schedule plus one-seventeenth thereof."

GLIDER CROSSES ATLANTIC

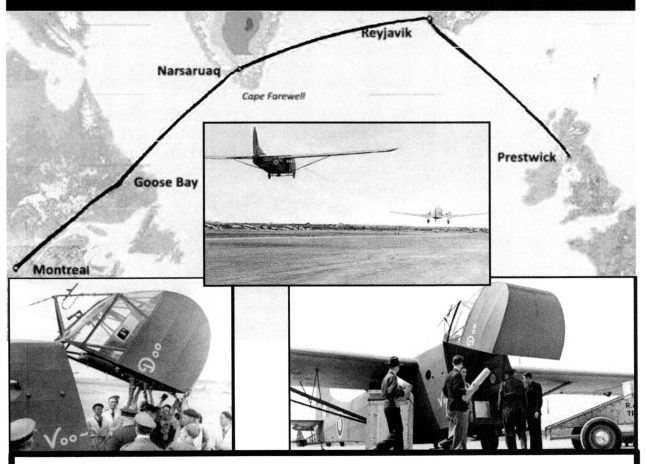

This week, a fully laden glider was towed across the Atlantic by RAF Transport Command. The idea of a transatlantic air freighter 'train' was conceived by Air Chief Marshal Sir Frederick Bowhill, of RAF Transport Command, who, while in charge of the North and South Atlantic Bomber Ferry from Canada, started experiments on the ultimate possibility of an Atlantic glider service for freight purposes. The glider, which has a wingspan of 84ft, was designed in the US and was fully laden with a ton and a half of war cargo including vaccines for Russia, radio, aircraft and motor parts, was towed by a Dakota, a twin-engine American aircraft.

On the journey from Montreal to Britain, weather conditions were mainly favourable, except that in the early stages a head wind made progress slow. After three hours flying the 'train' had reached a height of about 5,000ft trying to get above the clouds. When even at 13,000ft, the cloud bank towered above their heads, the pilots decided to descend and fly through the cloud instead. During the next three hours they came up against thunderstorms, ice and snow and the flyers were forced down to only 1,500 feet above ground. The trip was made in stages, with the glider reaching Britain exactly at the estimated time of arrival.

When the glider broke cloud over its destination, the towing aircraft was not visible, and it had the sky to itself whilst an interested group of spectators watched it make a perfect landing in the centre of the runway. Then the tug broke cloud, circled and dropped the towrope neatly at the appointed place, where an airman collected it - £80 worth of nylon. The tug landed and taxied to its station where a tractor delivered the glider alongside and within a few minutes the glider was unloaded.

AUGUST 1943

IN THE NEWS

WEEK 1

"Call Up Changes" Women up to the age of fifty are to be roped in for war work. Girls who could pass into one or other of the women's auxiliary services must now go into aircraft factories.

"Shortage of Partners" A 'rationing system' has been introduced in several north-west holiday towns for dance partners. Since the start of the holiday season there has been a great scarcity of men. At Blackpool there are ten women to one man.

WEEK 2

"Mosquitos Fly the Atlantic" Deliveries of Mosquitoes built in the Canadian De Havilland factory have begun. The all-wooden Mosquito has shown itself to be one of the RAF's most versatile machines. It is the fastest bomber ever built and can outpace any enemy fighter.

"End of Double Summertime" Clocks go back an hour over night. The reversion to ordinary summertime brings a much earlier black-out. The black-out will begin half an hour after sunset instead of three quarters of an hour.

WEEK 3

"Record Wings for Victory" The certified figures for all the Weeks show a total of £615,945,000 with 29.1% representing 'small savings.' Money from ordinary individuals.

"Last Night of the Proms" The Promenade Concerts ended with an all-British programme. Walton's 'Crown Imperial' March opened and Sir Henry Wood's, 'Fantasia on British Sea Songs' was the traditional ending.

WEEK 4

"Service in the Mines" Men of any age, if called up, can now enlist for service in the mines with the same right to demobilisation they would have if they enlisted in one of the fighting services.

HERE IN BRITAIN

"Queues for Work and Lodgers"

Amazing contrasts were seen around the country on this Bank Holiday. While at some seaside resorts crowded holidaymakers were queuing for something to eat and drink after sleeping all night in deck chairs on the prom, landladies at Blackpool were queuing up at the town's information bureau to ask for lodgers – and at one industrial town, holidaymakers were queuing up at a factory for work! It was a canning factory in Sheffield where an urgent call had gone out for helpers to deal with a glut of plums which would have gone bad if left over the holiday.

AROUND THE WORLD

"Presents for the United States"

The Coronation Scot, the famous British de-luxe train is among gifts to the US government from Britain, Canada, Cuba, Mexico, Venezuela, Brazil, Peru and other Central and South American countries as well as from every part of the US as well. The train, which millions of Americans viewed at the New York World's Fair, was a gift from LMS and is now in the service of the US Army. Other gifts include watches, bells, beans, beeswax, rubber, sugar, whisky, ambulances, aeroplanes, rifles, racing pigeons, German iron crosses, a sled complete with seven dog team and an antique shaving mug.

UNDERGROUND HEROES

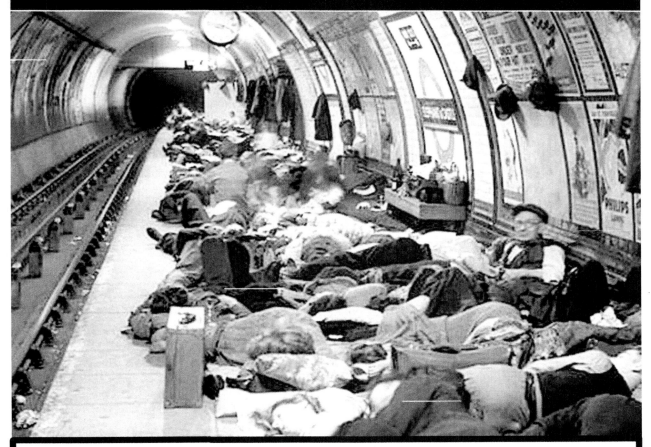

At the beginning of the war, the government was against people sheltering in the Underground tunnels during air raids. They feared that once people entered, they would be reluctant to come back above ground and continue normal life. More importantly, they were concerned that disease would spread due to the small number of toilets in some stations or that people would fall on the tube lines.

However, especially during the Blitz, when people began to force their way into the Underground stations and the arguments were proved wrong, the government changed its view and began kitting out some stations with bunks, first aid kits and chemical toilets. Night after night, just before the sirens sounded, thousands trooped down, taking their bedding with them, flasks of hot tea, snacks, radios, packs of cards and magazines. People had their regular places and set up little communities.

However, Underground stations are not completely safe as bomb shelters – they are still vulnerable to a direct hit and a high explosive bomb can penetrate up to fifty feet through solid ground. When a small bomb scored a direct hit on the Marble Arch subway, filled with people in September 1940, its blast ripped the white tiles off the walls and made them deadly projectiles killing twenty people.

The most destructive incident happened in October 1940 at Balham station when a 1400 kg fragmentation bomb fell on the road above the northern end of the platform tunnels, creating a large crater into which a double decker bus then crashed. The northbound platform tunnel partially collapsed and was filled with earth and water from the fractured water mains and sewers above. Although more than 400 managed to escape, 68 people died in the disaster. Many were drowned as water and sewage from burst mains poured in.

SEPTEMBER 1943

IN THE NEWS

WEEK 1

"National Observance Day" In the smallest villages as in London and other cities, in military camps and arms factories, in shops and harvest fields, there was a brief break for an act of worship on the fourth anniversary of Britain's entry into the war.

"More Rail Bars" To provide a means by which passengers can obtain snacks to take with them on trains, at non-terminal stations, a distinct 'compact' design of Rail Bar has been adopted by the LMS. The first is at Crewe and others are being opened at Preston, Derby, Sheffield, and Rugby.

WEEK 2

"Call Up Deferments to End" In view of the urgent need for men in the forces, the Government has decided that deferments granted for qualifying men in munitions and other industries must end.

"First Woman MP in Australia" Dame Enid Lyons, widow of the late Prime Minister of Australia, has won Darwin, Tasmania, for the United Australia Party in the recent election and become the first woman to enter the House of Representatives.

WEEK 3

"Rural Workers Cottages" The Minister of Health opened the first two cottages built under the emergency rural housing scheme. Built in just 11 weeks which is a creditable enough achievement in peace-time, and remarkable under war-time conditions.

WEEK 4

"Brighter Torches" You no longer need to dim torches with a piece of newspaper, though the light shown is still limited to a circle one inch in diameter, because, to economise with batteries, flash lamp bulbs will in future be of a lower amperage.

HERE IN BRITAIN

"Hard Work with Stretchers"

RAMC orderlies, stretcher bearers and the like must be A1 men to do stretcher work in the field. All training centres have the 'best assault course' and cadets go round the obstacles carrying a badly wounded man firmly strapped to a stretcher.

They pull him through long, dark tunnels with live ammunition going off all around; over tall walls and through and over piles of loose wood; drop him down high cliffs and carry him back up again and take him through fire and smoke. Carrying a wounded man of average weight, with his full kit, over this obstacle course, needs perfect physical condition.

AROUND THE WORLD

"Pyrethrum Seed from Kenya"

Kenya has become the world's principal source of supply of pyrethrum seed and 20,000 lb is now being collected for delivery to Russia in November to replant 7,500 acres of war devastated Caucasian field which previously grew pyrethrum.

Recently, 10,000 lb was sent to Brazil and other recent consignments include 5,000 lb to India and smaller quantities to Egypt, Australia, Nyasaland, Nigeria, Ceylon, Jamaica and the Belgian Congo. The country thus provides one of the most important allied war supplies, among the uses of which are a protection for troops against malaria in tropical countries and a preservative of stored foods.

MAKING MORE FROM LESS

An exhibition by the Ministry of Supply, illustrates the ingenuity, resource and inventive skill which have been employed to make good the loss of oversea imports. Production has been trebled since 1940 although the import of raw materials has halved. New materials, new designs, and new methods of manufacture have all contributed to the result, necessity having proved the prolific mother of invention.

Some changes have been simple. A new design of cotton reel which saves 6,000 tons of wood a year; solid wood lapping boards used by drapers as a core for rolls of fabric are now a frame covered with paper saving 50,000 tons of wood a year; slats instead of solid seats in barrack room forms have saved 1,815,000 cu ft of timber.

In producing munitions, the electric forging of six-pounder armour-piercing shells entirely abolishes waste and for shells from 25-pounders to the 9.2 howitzers a new method of forging has saved 400,000 tons of steel and 18,000,000 man-hours of work. The recuperator block of a 25-pounder gun, when made of welded tubes, is 900lb lighter than the old solid forging. An auxiliary aircraft petrol tank to be jettisoned is being made of paper and landing wheel fairings for fighters of fibre. A new process for rifle barrels was not shown to save materials, but the manpower which formerly produced two now produces 100.

The new bayonet of fabricated parts saves 60% labour and 50% steel. Plastic is taking the place of metal in the nose caps of shells and 2,000 tons of brass a year are saved by making regimental badges and buttons of plastic. During the last year over 1,000,000 pairs of Army boots have been returned to service with a saving of 7s (35p) a pair, and because 'broken in' they are described as 'better than new.'

OCTOBER 1943

IN THE NEWS

WEEK 1 "£25 Million Raised" In the first four years of the war, the many Red Cross and St John War Organisations have benefited greatly since repatriated prisoners of war have told of lives being saved by Red Cross parcels.

WEEK 2 "Prisoners' Toys" Toys are being made from wood salvaged from blitzed buildings, by inmates in 15 prisons. They provide rocking horses, railway engines, wheelbarrows, blackboards and easels urgently needed by the Nursery School Association.

"Oranges" Eighty-four million oranges have arrived in the country from South Africa and every child up to the age of 16 will have a share.

WEEK 3 "Switch for Winter Production" Munitions production has been switched from basic items such as guns and ammunition to an emphasis on invasion craft, bridging materials, cranes, and needs for rapid movement of armies by land, sea or air.

"Emigration to Australia" The Australian Government is examining the prospects of assisted immigration on a large scale from the UK after the war. They believe there is ample scope for the employment of workers from British industry.

WEEK 4 "Greatest Harvest in History" More land has been given up for aerodromes, battle training grounds and such like, so we have grown a record amount of food from the smallest acreage devoted since records began.

"The USS Lafayette Ready for Refitting" The salving of the former French liner 'Normandie', which caught fire in New York Harbour in February last year, has been completed and she is to be refitted as a transport vessel.

HERE IN BRITAIN
"Wakey Wakey"

For nearly three years the sound of an alarm clock has not been heard in the Leeds district and timekeeping has not been the same since the 'knockers up' joined up. When, four months ago, there was mention of 60,000 American alarm clocks arriving, essential workers clapped each other on the back - and when the clocks failed to materialise, they took it with Yorkshire stoicism.

Recently another few thousand clocks were expected and 4,000 workers applied for permits. It was computed that Leeds should get at least six of them, but never a clock, never a permit has made its appearance.

AROUND THE WORLD
"Little Ship's Long Voyage"

A captain in the Merchant Navy, took an egg-shaped, 300-ton crane-ship, 15,200 miles, including a passage round the Cape, to Turkey. The voyage was an extraordinary feat of navigation, as the ship, called 'Turkish Delight' by the crew, was built exclusively for use in sheltered waters and is only 10ft long.

She was so difficult to steer that for months it was thought that she would never be able to leave the Clyde. Yet for 10 months she was taken, unescorted, through gales, heavy seas, and waters in which enemy U-boats were operating and was delivered safely.

ROYAL OBSERVER CORPS

The Royal Observer Corps is nearly 30 years old, is some 40,000 strong, and has been doing a vital front-line job every second of the day and night since a week before the outbreak of the present war. Briefly, their main task is to spot and plot the course of every aircraft, both hostile and friendly, which is over or approaching these shores. Throughout Britain there are 1,500 carefully sited observer posts, each manned every minute of the 24 hours by two highly trained observers. They are liable to have any one of nearly 300 types of friendly and hostile aircraft over their posts which are often situated in outlandish spots, on a hill or a headland, on top of a church tower or even on top of a tree in a pine wood.

They are manned day and night in every type of weather, and the spotters 'tell' every outgoing or incoming aircraft by direct telephone line to the nearest ROC centre, of which there are 40 conveniently scattered about the country. Here there is a table like those in use in Fighter operations rooms, on which the course of the aircraft is plotted. The centre in its turn keeps Fighter Command abreast of the situation and is an ever-present means for the RAF to keep a constant check on any developments. It is on information from the men and women of ROC that air raid warnings are sounded.

For security reasons the public have heard little of the ROC, they have not heard, for instance, of the countless lives which have been saved by ROC information on 'homing' crippled bombers returning from the Continent, nor of the many lives saved by alerting Air-Sea rescue to aircraft down in the sea.

NOVEMBER 1943

IN THE NEWS

WEEK 1 "Slag Heaps on Football Pitches" The war time increase in coal production in the narrow valleys of South Wales has meant slag heaps are growing and spreading too quickly. In some places Rugby football pitches, cherished as precious communal possessions, are being threatened.

WEEK 2 "Anniversary of the Soviet Union" The twenty-fifth anniversary was celebrated in London at the Stoll Theatre. The Dean of Canterbury resided and said, *"we are present to congratulate Russia on what she has done. After the enemy has been vanquished, we should together enter on the task of building up a new world."*

"Golden Arrow" The Royal Signals have a new, mobile, high-speed wireless station for keeping armies in the field in touch with GHQ and the War Office. It is named after the famous London-Paris boat-train because troops and equipment are carried in long train-like motor-vehicles.

WEEK 3 "Save Your Tyres" The manufacture of synthetic rubber in America has not reduced the need for economy. The largest consumption of rubber is for large tyres on omnibuses, lorries and aeroplanes and crude rubber will still be needed.

"Uproar at Mosley's Release" The Home Secretary has announced that Sir Oswald Mosley, the man who introduced Fascism to Britain, is to be released from Holloway prison where he has been held since 1940, on medical grounds.

WEEK 4 "Thanksgiving Day" For the second year in succession, the Stars and Stripes flew over Westminster Abbey whilst, inside, hundreds of Americans celebrated Thanksgiving Day.

HERE IN BRITAIN

"Civilians Leave the South-West"

Removal of the population has begun in the area where 3,000 people must leave their homes before the end of December to make room for a battle training ground for the United States Army. Some of the inhabitants did not yet know where they were going or when they will be able to return to their homes and farms.

The area includes 200 farms and must be completely cleared. An American general told one gathering *"The hardship you are suffering will be compensated by the lives of Americans and Britishers that will be saved by what the men learn during their training in this area."*

AROUND THE WORLD

"Goodbye Bully"

The Australian Army catering service has been working on an improved substitute for 'bully and biscuit' which is more palatable, more nourishing, and even more portable. The new ration is contained in an air-tight tin eight by four by two inches which when opened can be used as a billy. Inside are three packages each weighing 1lb, representing one complete meal and sealed in waterproof paper.

Two packages a day adequately maintain one soldier in the field. Each package also contains four tea tablets, two sugar tablets, two salt tablets and skim milk powder. Gaps in the packages are filled with barley sugar.

SPIRIDONOVKA PALACE

The Third Moscow Conference between the major Allies, where the Moscow Declaration was issued, took place at the Kremlin but the delegates also met at the Spiridonovka Palace in Moscow. This Palace was built by an eccentric called Arseny Morozon, the younger son of a Moscow textile 'king'. Born into great wealth, he was uninterested in his father's business, leaving that to an equally eccentric, prolific art collecting, older brother, and young Arseny engaged in a hedonistic life, indulging his greatest passions, hunting and dog-breeding. In the late 1890's he was consumed with an additional passion, building a Gothic-Moorish castle next to his mother's classical mansion on Volkhonka Street, on a plot she offered him on his 25th birthday. Inspired by the faux-medieval Pena Palace in Portugal, Arseny reproduced that mishmash of styles, adding a facade copied from the House of Shells in Salamanca. The building provoked widespread ridicule even before it was completed, being absurdly out of place in central Moscow. Tolstoy, in his book 'The Resurrection' has a passer-by describe the building as a *'stupid unnecessary palace for a stupid useless person'*.

If the exterior was eccentric, the interior decoration followed suit, reflecting an absolute eclecticism of styles. From pseudo-Gothic to Empire, from Arabic to Chinese, the Palace is filled with carved woodwork, Persian carpets, brocade hangings, marble mantelpieces, white and gold, satin upholstered, Empire furniture and stained glass. After the Revolution, the Palace became the theatre, 'Proletkult' until 1928, then the embassy of different countries and even the editions of British newspapers and is now the Reception House for the Soviet Foreign Minister. In the Music Room, where the meetings probably took place, hangs a painting presented by the British Government of Anthony Eden signing, in the presence of Churchill, Molotov and Maisky, the Anglo Soviet Treaty of May last year.

DECEMBER 1943

IN THE NEWS

WEEK 1   **"Men For the Mines Compulsion"** Because voluntary recruitment measures have not worked, the Government has decided that some thousands of men between 18 and 25, who would otherwise go to the services, must now be 'directed' to the mines.

"Death to London Sewer Rats" An onslaught against the brown rats begins today. Rats have been damaging food to the extent of 2,000,000 tons a year.

WEEK 2   **"Help from Army Doctors"** The Ministry of Health is securing more medical aid to deal with the influenza epidemic. The call up of young doctors has been delayed and Service medical officers are to help.

"Cancer Cure Will Save Thousands" For the first time in history, it is possible to state that one form of cancer, cancer of the prostate, can be completely controlled and the patient rendered symptom free by taking a few pills each day.

WEEK 3   **"The First Ballot"** A junior member of staff at the Ministry of Labour drew the first two numbers in the ballot for the direction of young men to the coal mines. The first training sessions will begin in January.

WEEK 4   **"Mrs Churchill Flies Across War Zone"** There has been no spread in his pneumonia and the improvement in the Prime Minister's health has been maintained. Clementine Churchill, his wife, has braved a cold and dangerous flight to be at his side in Cairo.

"Postcards Arrived in Time" Some 13,000 postcards from prisoners of war and civilian internees in Japanese hands reached this country in time for delivery by Christmas. The majority came from Malaya.

HERE IN BRITAIN
"Airgraphs Going Nowhere"

The airgraph letter service has created trouble for the postal authorities. Each week the GPO is receiving some 2,000 airgraphs bearing no address, 210 stamped and addressed but without any message, and 150 properly stamped forms, 3d or 8d, with no word written on them!

The other frequent mistakes are folding the forms unnecessarily small, usually into eight, meaning they must be smoothed out before going through the photographing machines or sticking a photograph of themselves or the baby on the form which makes it too thick for the machine.

AROUND THE WORLD
"Kissing the Sword of Stalingrad"

This week the King's sword was presented to Marshal Joseph Stalin by Mr Churchill, in the presence of President Roosevelt, at a ceremony during the Teheran Conference. Churchill took the sword and turning to Stalin declared, *"I am commanded to present this sword of honour as a token of homage of the British people"*.

Stalin kissed the scabbard and quietly thanked the British. He then offered the sword for inspection to the seated President who drew the blade and held it aloft, saying, *"Truly they had hearts of steel"*. (In Russian, Stalin's name approximates to 'man of steel').

BEVIN'S 'BOYS' BALLOT

Training in the highly dangerous coal industry was taken seriously. The Bevin's Boys had both theoretical and practical training in underground coal mining.

Mr Bevin has decided the young men, aged 18 – 25, to be called up for the mines should be selected by ballot. A draw will be made from time to time of one or more of the numbers from 0 to 9, and those men eligible, whose National Service registration certificates happen to end with the figure or figures drawn, will be transferred to the coalmines. 30,000 men are needed before the end of next April.

If your name is called out of the hat, this is what will happen. You will be given at least four weeks training. 50% of your 44-hour week will be spent in physical training and classroom work, 30% on instruction below ground and the remaining 20% on surface work. An experienced miner will supervise your work during the first four weeks underground and unless you live in South Wales, you will not be sent to work at the coal face until you have had at least four months underground experience. You will be billeted in a miner's home or in a specially built hostel. You will receive a minimum wage ranging from 39s 6d (£1.97) at 17, to 78s (£3.40) at 21, with allowances for living away from home and when demobilisation comes, you will be dealt with exactly as though you were a soldier. Three classes of men will be excluded. Men accepted for flying duties in the RAF or Fleet Air Arm; men accepted as artificers in submarines and men in a short list of highly skilled occupations. Conscientious objectors will not be exempt.

The President of the South Wales miners said, "I think the plan will work. It will get rid of the idea that young men who have volunteered for the mines, have done so to avoid military service."

1940:

Jan: Britain calls up 2 million 19 to 27-year-olds for military service.

Jan: Food rationing is introduced in Britain

May: Winston Churchill becomes PM.

Jul: Battle of Britain begins.

1941:

May: Nine months of intensive Blitz bombing ends.

May: First British jet aircraft, the Gloster, is flown.

Jun: Clothes rationing introduced in Britain.

1942:

Feb: The Fall of Singapore to the Japanese.

Feb: Soap rationing introduced in Britain.

Oct: British sailors board a German submarine as it sinks in the Mediterranean and retrieve its Enigma machine and codebooks

Nov: General Montgomery's Eighth Army wins the Second Battle of El Alamein.

1943:

Jan: Utility furniture first becomes available.

May: The 'Dambuster Raid' breaches German dams in the Ruhr Valley.

Dec: First 'Bevin Boys' selected from conscripts to work in the coal mines.

1944:

Feb: PAYE (pay as you earn) system of tax collection introduced.

Jun: D-Day for the Normandy landings. 155,000 Allied troops land on the beaches of France

Dec: The Home Guard is stood down.

1940: Between 26 May and 4 June, the evacuation from Dunkirk of the British Expeditionary Force takes place. 300,000 troops are evacuated, many by little private boats, from France to England.

1941: In February, the luxury liner RMS Queen Elizabeth, now fitted with anti-aircraft guns and with her hull repainted begins her first voyage as a troopship out of Singapore.

1945:

May: Victory in Europe is declared. Celebrations take place throughout Britain. Prime Minister Winston Churchill makes a victory speech.

Jun: The demobilisation of the wartime forces begins.

1946:

May: London Heathrow Airport is opened fully for civilian use.

Jun: The BBC resumes television broadcasting, suspended during the war. Licences are introduced.

Aug: Family allowance cash benefits to mothers are introduced and daily free milk to school children.

1947:

Jan: The Government nationalises the Coal Industry.

Apr: The school leaving age is raised from 14 to 15.

Sep: The University of Cambridge votes to allow women to become full students.

1948:

Jan: The Government nationalises the Railway industry.

Jul: The National Health Service begins, giving the right to universal, free, healthcare.

Jul & Aug: The Olympic Games are held in London.

1949:

Jan: Peacetime conscription in Britain begins. Men aged 18-26 must serve full-time in the armed forces for 18 months.

Jul: The de Havilland Comet, the world's first passenger jet, makes its maiden flight.

1947: The winter was one of the harshest experienced in the British Isles and February was exceptionally cold with heavy snowfalls. It was the coldest February of the century with an average of −1.9 °C (28.6 °F).

1947: In November, Princess Elizabeth marries Philip Mountbatten at Westminster Abbey. The ceremony was broadcast live on BBC television, without sound. The commentary was provided from the studio.

1943 THE WAR

January
27th 50 bombers mount the first all American air raid against Germany. Wilhelmshaven, the large naval base, is the primary target.

February
11th U.S. General Dwight D. Eisenhower is selected to command the Allied armies in Europe.

March
5th : Essen is bombed, marking the beginning of a four-month attack on the Ruhr industrial area.
13th German forces liquidate the Jewish ghetto in Kraków.
17th Devastating convoy losses in the Atlantic due to increased U-boat activity.

April
19th The Warsaw Ghetto uprising: On the Eve of Passover, Jews resist German attempts to deport the Jewish community.
28th : Allies attempt to close the mid-Atlantic gap in the war against the U-boats with long-range bombers.

May
15th The French form a "Resistance Movement".
16th The Warsaw Ghetto Uprising ends. The ghetto has been destroyed, with about 14,000 Jews killed and 40,000 sent to the death camps at Majdanek and Treblinka.
16th The Dambuster Raids are carried out by RAF 617 Squadron on two German dams, Mohne and Eder. The Ruhr war industries lose electrical power.
24th Admiral Karl Dönitz orders the majority of U-boats to withdraw from the Atlantic because of heavy losses to new Allied anti-submarine tactics.
29th RAF bombs Wuppertal, causing heavy civilian losses.

July
7th Walter Dornberger briefs the V-2 rocket to Hitler, who approves the project for top priority.
24th Hamburg, Germany, is heavily bombed in Operation Gomorrah, which at the time is the heaviest assault in the history of aviation.

August
29th During the Occupation of Denmark by Nazi Germany, martial law replaced the Danish government.

September
3rd Nazi Germany begins the evacuation of civilians from Berlin.
22nd British midget submarines attack the German battleship Tirpitz, at anchor in a Norwegian fjord, crippling her for six months.
30th Danes are secretly sending their Jewish countrymen to Sweden by boat crossings.

October
4th Corsica is liberated by Free French forces.
19th The German War Office contracts the Mittelwerk to produce 12,000 V-2 rockets.
22/23rd An air raid on Kassel causes a seven-day firestorm.

November
9th General De Gaulle becomes President of the French Committee of National Liberation.
27th Huge civilian losses in Berlin as heavy bombing raids continue.

December
14th United States XV Corps arrives in European Theatre.
24th US General Dwight D. Eisenhower becomes the Supreme Allied Commander in Europe.
26th German battleship *Scharnhorst* is sunk off North Cape (in the Arctic) by a British force led by the battleship HMS *Duke of York*.
27th General Eisenhower is officially named head of Overlord, the invasion of Normandy.

SUMMARY
1943 saw Germany in control of continental Europe, occupying from France in the west, to Italy in the south and east to Russia. However the tide was starting to turn with greater resistance from occupied people and increasingly heavy Allied bombing raids over German cities and industrial areas.

In Western Europe

The RAF Dambusters

The British Air Ministry had identified the industrialised Ruhr Valley, especially its dams, as important strategic targets. The dams provided hydroelectric power and pure water for steel-making, drinking water and water for the canal transport system. A one-off surprise attack might succeed but the RAF lacked a weapon suitable for the task. The mission grew out of a concept for a large barrel shaped bomb designed by Barnes Wallis. The bomb would skip across the surface of the water before hitting the dam wall and then run down the side of the dam towards its base, thus maximising the explosive effect against the dam.

The targets selected were the Möhne Dam and the Sorpe Dam, upstream from the Ruhr industrial area, with the Eder Dam on the Eder River as a secondary target.

On the night of 6/17 May, 19 Lancaster bombers took off flying at a very low altitude, just above wave height to avoid detection. One struck the sea, one an electricity pylon and one was shot down over Holland. Five bombers reached the Möhne dam and four dropped their bombs with the last breaching the dam wall.
Three bombers reached the Eder dam and they successfully breached the dam. The attacks on the Sorpe and Ennepe Dams were unsuccessful. On the way back, flying again at treetop level, two more Lancasters were lost meaning only eleven out of the original eighteen survived.

The Möhne and Edersee dams were breached, causing catastrophic flooding of the Ruhr valley Two hydroelectric power stations were destroyed . Factories and mines were also damaged and destroyed. An estimated 1,600 civilians — about 600 Germans and 1,000 forced labourers, mainly Soviet — were killed by the flooding. Despite rapid repairs by the Germans, production did not return to normal until September. The RAF lost 53 aircrew killed and 3 captured, with 8 aircraft destroyed.

1943 THE WAR

January

10th Soviet troops launch an all-out offensive attack on Stalingrad

21st The last airfield at Stalingrad is taken by Red Army forces, ensuring that the Luftwaffe will be unable to supply German troops any further.

24th German forces in Stalingrad are in the last phases of collapse.

February

2nd The Soviet Union, the Battle of Stalingrad comes to an end with the official surrender of the German 6th Army.

March

13th German forces liquidate the Jewish ghetto in Kraków.

14th Germans recapture Kharkov.

16th The first reports of the Katyn massacre in Poland seep to the West; reports say that more than 22,000 prisoners of war were killed by the NKVD (Russian Political Police), who eventually blame the massacre on the Germans.

April

15th Finland officially rejects Soviet terms for peace.

July

12th The Battle of Prokhorovka begins the largest tank battle in human history and part of the Battle of Kursk, it is the pivotal battle of Operation Citadel.

13th Hitler calls off the Kursk offensive, but the Soviets continue the battle.

August

5th Swedish government announces it will no longer allow German troops and war material to transit Swedish railways.

5th Russians recapture Orel and Belgorod.

23rd Operation Polkovodets Rumyantsev liberates Kharkov, Ukraine. The Battle of Kursk has become the first successful major

Belongings abandoned as Jews are cleared from Krakow

September

4th Soviet Union declares war on Bulgaria.

25th The Red Army retakes Smolensk.

November

6th The Red Army liberates the city of Kiev. This is an anniversary of the Russian Revolution in 1917.

16th Kalinin is retaken in a large Red Army offensive.

26th The Red Army offensive in the Ukraine continues.

Stalin, Roosevelt and Churchill meet to discuss war strategy.

SUMMARY

1943 sees the Russian Red army inflict successive heavy losses on the German army. Stalingrad is regained, cutting off supplies to the German troops who are pushed back west. Russia start to occupy the Ukraine and some Baltic states and advance in Bulgaria. For the first time, Germany is in retreat.

ON THE RUSSIAN FRONT

THE BATTLE FOR STALINGRAD

The Germans had reached Stalingrad in August 1942. By October 1942 90% of Stalingrad was destroyed, and all civilians were manning the defences. The Germans has almost complete control but in November much of the German air force was sent away to help in North Africa and the freezing weather caught the Germans unprepared and ill-equipped. The Russians started to counter attack and surrounded the German force.

The Germans tried to evacuate their troops and by 18 December were only 30ml from Stalingrad but were ordered back. The military and political leadership of Nazi Germany sought not to relieve them, but to get them to fight on for as long as possible so as to tie up the Soviet forces.

The Red Army offered the Germans a chance to surrender on 7 January 1943. If they surrendered within 24 hours, there would be a guarantee of safety for all prisoners, medical care for the sick and wounded, prisoners being allowed to keep their personal belongings, "normal" food rations, and repatriation to any country they wished after the war. Hitler rejected this offer.

The Germans were now not only starving but running out of ammunition. Nevertheless, they continued to resist, in part because they believed the Soviets would execute any who surrendered.

On 22 January, Russia once again offered Paulus, the German commander, a chance to surrender. He told Hitler that he was no longer able to command his men, who were without ammunition or food. Hitler rejected this surrender on a point of honour. On 31st January 1943, the 10th anniversary of Hitler's coming to power Soviet forces reached the entrance to the German headquarters. Around 91,000 exhausted, ill, wounded, and starving prisoners were taken. The prisoners included 22 generals. The battle was over. On 2nd February.

The Axis suffered 747,300 – 868,374 combat casualties (killed, wounded or captured) among all branches of the German armed forces and their allies. The Germans lost 900 aircraft, 500 tanks and 6,000 artillery pieces. The USSR, suffered 1,129,619 total casualties; 478,741 personnel killed or missing, and 650,878 wounded or sick. The USSR lost 4,341 tanks destroyed or damaged, 15,728 artillery pieces and 2,769 combat aircraft.

January

15th The British start an offensive aimed at taking Tripoli, Libya.

23th British capture Tripoli, Libya

February

2nd Rommel retreats farther into Tunisia. Within two days, Allied troops move into Tunisia for the first time.

5th The Allies now have all of Libya under their control.

8th : United States' VI Corps arrives in North Africa.

13th Rommel launches a counter-attack against the Americans in western Tunisia; he takes Sidi Bouzid and Gafsa. The Battle of the Kasserine Pass begins: inexperienced American troops are soon forced to retreat.

March

6th Battle of Medenine, Tunisia. It is Rommel's last battle in Africa as he is forced to retreat.

18th General George S. Patton leads his tanks of II Corps into Gafsa, Tunisia.

20th Montgomery's forces begin a breakthrough in Tunisia, striking at the Mareth line.

23th American tanks defeat the Germans at El Guettar, Tunisia.

26th The British break through the Mareth line in southern Tunisia, threatening the whole German army. The Germans move north.

April

7th Hitler and Mussolini come together at Salzburg, mostly for the purpose of propping up Mussolini's fading morale.

Allied forces–the Americans from the West, the British from the East–link up near Gafsa in Tunisia.

May

7th Tunis captured by British First Army. Meanwhile, the Americans take Bizerte.

13th Remaining German Afrika Korps and Italian troops in North Africa surrender to Allied forces. The Allies take over 250,000 prisoners

22nd Allies bomb Sicily and Sardinia, both possible landing sites.

31st American B-17's bomb Naples.

June

11th British 1st Division takes the Italian island of Pantelleria, between Tunisia and Sicily, capturing 11,000 Italian troops.

12th The Italian island of Lampedusa, between Tunisia and Sicily, surrenders to the Allies.

July

10th The Allied invasion of Sicily begins.

19th The Allies bomb Rome for the first time

22nd U.S. forces under Patton capture Palermo, Sicily

August

6th German troops start to take over Italy's defences.

11th German and Italian forces begin to evacuate Sicily.

17th All of Sicily now controlled by the Allies.

September

3rd A secret Italian Armistice is signed and Italy drops out of the war. Mainland Italy is invaded when the British XXIII Corps lands at Reggio Calabria.

8th Eisenhower publicly announces the surrender of Italy to the Allies.

9th The Allies land at Salerno, Italy.

10th German troops occupy Rome. The Italian fleet surrenders at Malta and other Mediterranean ports.

28th The people of Naples, sensing the approach of the Allies, rise up against the German occupiers.

October

1st Neapolitans complete their uprising and free Naples from German military occupation.

13th Italy declares war on Germany.

November

5th The Vatican is bombed in a failed attempt to knock out the Vatican radio.

SUMMARY

1943 saw strong Allied gains in all regions. By May, the Allies had captured N. Africa and over 250,000 prisoners. The campaign to free Italy started and soon had taken Sicily with the Italians on the run, so much so that Hitler sent his own troops in to fight instead of the Italians. Italy eventually declared war on Germany!

Montgomery talks to British troops near Catania

British troops scramble over a devastated street in Catania, Sicily, 5 August 1943.

ALLIES CAPTURE SICILY

Sicily was defended by 200,000 Italian troops, 70,000 German troops and 30,000 *Luftwaffe* ground staff. The German commanders in Sicily were contemptuous of their allies and German units took their orders from Generalfeldmarschall Albert Kesselring.

The night of 9–10 July, just south of Syracuse, was the start of the joint American and British invasion. Strong winds blew 69 gliders off course, crashing into the sea, with over 200 men drowning. Landings were made the same night on 26 main beaches of the southern and eastern coasts of the island . This was the largest amphibious operation of World War II. The Italian defensive plan did not contemplate large beach landings so the Allies encountered no major resistance.

By 27 July, the Axis commanders had realised that the Italians and Germans would retreat to the Italian mainland through the port of Messina. Organised by the Germans the full-scale withdrawal began on 11 August and continued to 17 August. The Germans made successive withdrawals each night of between 8 and 24 kilometres (5 and 15 miles), keeping the following Allied units at arm's length with the use of mines, demolitions and other obstacles and despite the Allies attempting to counter this the evacuation proved highly successful.

The Italians evacuated 62,182 men, 41 guns and 227 vehicles. The Germans evacuated some 52,000 troops. The Allies had taken Sicily in a month with over 22,000 casualties (5,700 killed or missing, 16,000 wounded, and 3,300 captured), while the Germans lost 8,900 men killed or missing, 5,532 captured and 13,500 wounded, with Italian military losses of 40,700 killed or missing, 32,500 wounded and 116,681 captured.

1943 THE WAR

January

2nd Americans and Australians recapture Buna, New Guinea.

February

8th The Chindits (a "long range penetration group") under British General Orde Wingate begin an incursion into Burma.

9th Guadalcanal is finally secured; it is the first major victory of the American offensive in the Pacific war.

18th Chindits under Wingate cut the railway line between Mandalay and Myitkyina.

21st Americans take the Russell Islands, part of the Solomons chain.

April

4th The only large-scale escape of Allied prisoners-of-war from the Japanese in the Pacific takes place when ten American POWs and two Filipino convicts break out of the Davao Penal Colony on the island of Mindanao in the southern Philippines. The escaped POWs were the first to break the news of the infamous Bataan Death March and other atrocities committed by the Japanese, to the world.

May

2nd Japanese aircraft again bomb Darwin, Australia.

11th American and Canadian troops invade Attu Island in the Aleutian Islands in an attempt to expel occupying Japanese forces.

30th Attu Island is again under American control.

June

8th Japanese forces begin to evacuate Kiska Island in the Aleutians, their last foothold in the West.

21st American troops land in the Trobriand Islands, close to New Guinea. The American strategy of driving up the Southwest Pacific by "Island Hopping" continues.

22nd The Cairo Conference: US President Franklin D. Roosevelt, British Prime Minister Winston Churchill, and ROC leader Chiang Kai-shek meet in Cairo, Egypt, to discuss ways to defeat Japan.

25th Rangoon is bombed by American heavy bombers.

July

6th U.S. and Japanese ships fight the Battle of Kula Gulf in the Solomons.

August

6th Japan declares independence for the State of Burma under Dr. Ba Maw.

6/7th The U.S. wins the Battle of Vella in the Solomons.

September

21st The battle of the Solomons can now be considered at an unofficial end.

22nd Australian forces land at Finschhafen, a small port in New Guinea. The Japanese continue the battle well into October.

October

3rd Churchill appoints Lord Louis Mountbatten the commander of South East Asia Command.

7th The Japanese execute 98 American civilians on Wake Island.

November

1st In Operation Goodtime, United States Marines land on Bougainville in the Solomon Islands. The fighting on this island will continue to the end of the war.

20: US Marines land on Tarawa and the American public is shocked by the heavy losses suffered by their forces.

December

29th Control of the Andaman Islands is handed over to Azad Hind by the Japanese.

SUMMARY

1943 saw the Allied forces slowly gain naval and air supremacy in the Pacific. They moved methodically from island to island, conquering them one at a time despite sustaining significant casualties.

The Japanese, however, successfully defended their positions on the Chinese mainland and much of SE Asia until 1945.

IN ASIA AND THE PACIFIC

Japanese school girls wave off a Kamikaze pilot (top).

American aircraft carrier USS Bunker Hill burns after being hit by two kamikaze planes (Bottom right).

US Marines advancing (Bottom left)

THE ISLAND HOPPING STRATEGY

Leapfrogging, also known as island hopping, was a military strategy employed by the Allies in the Pacific War against the Empire of Japan during World War II. The key idea is to bypass heavily fortified enemy islands instead of trying to capture every island in sequence en route to a final target. The reasoning is that those islands can simply be cut off from their supply chains (leading to their eventual capitulation) rather than needing to be overwhelmed by superior force, thus speeding up progress and reducing losses of troops and material. This would allow the United States forces to reach Japan quickly and not expend the time, manpower, and supplies to capture every Japanese-held island on the way. It would give the Allies the advantage of surprise and keep the Japanese off balance.

This strategy was possible in part because the Allies used submarine and air attacks to blockade and isolate Japanese bases, weakening their garrisons and reducing the Japanese ability to resupply and reinforce them. Thus troops on islands which had been bypassed, such as the major base at Rabaul, were useless to the Japanese war effort and left to "wither on the vine". This strategy began to be implemented in late 1943 in Operation Cartwheel. MacArthur's Operation Cartwheel, Operation Reckless and Operation Persecution were the first successful Allied practices of leapfrogging in terms of landing on lightly guarded beaches and very low casualties but cutting off Japanese troops hundreds of miles away from their supply routes.

THE HOME

This decade could be divided into two, up until 1945 and the post-war years. Home life during the war years was very austere and drab and for many, empty, if their children had been evacuated to a safer part of the country. Jobs that before only men would do, women were now doing. Homes were protected with sandbags against explosives; windows were covered with blackout blinds and there were Anderson shelters in gardens. During the whole decade, people listened to the radio, but many people also had gramophones to play 78rpm records.

The war songs remained popular with Vera Lynn a favourite, together with the big bands, swing, jazz and country music from America. Towards the end of the decade, the crooners like Bing Crosby and Frank Sinatra were taking precedence.

Clothes rationing ended in 1954 but materials were still scarce, and fashion was not feasible for millions of women trying to forge a new life after the deprivations of the war.

For those who did, Dior's 'New Look' made the 'hourglass' the shape to aspire to. Skirt suits were popular, with squared shoulders, a narrow waist and tailored skirt that ended just below the knee, and hats, gloves and bright red lipstick, completed an outfit.

Even when the war ended in 1945, much of the rationing continued. Linoleum was still the king of floor coverings, with a rug in 'the front room'; thousands of families relied on a tin bath in the kitchen for their weekly bath and the toilet was located outside in the garden. 'Colour' was in short supply. BBC television programmes were resumed in 1946 but TV ownership was extremely low and the wireless reigned supreme.

After the war, families did not 'eat out', meals were cooked and served at home, usually to the whole family around one table. Without supermarkets, the woman of the house, shopped at individual butchers, bakers and grocers and the food available was limited and seasonal.

The 'Make do and Mend' mentality endured and during the 1940s you would be hard pressed to find a woman who didn't know how to knit. Lace and airy stitch patterns were a great way to make a little yarn go a long way and it wasn't just wool that was in limited supply, dyes were scarce which meant that colours were limited too.

1940:

The BBC Forces Programme begins broadcasting and becomes the most popular channel among civilians at home as well. **Music While You Work** begins in June.

King George VI announces the creation of the George Cross decoration during a radio broadcast. Ealing Studio release the war comedy **Sailors Three.** The song, **All Over the Place** becomes one of the most popular of the war.

A revival of John Gay's **The Beggar's Opera** directed by John Gielgud opens at the Haymarket.

1941:

Noël Coward's comedy **Blithe Spirit** is premiered at Manchester and opens in London in July and becomes an instant success.

The first Ronald Searle cartoon to feature **St Trinian's School** is published in the magazine Lilliput.

London's Queen's Hall, the venue for the **Promenade Concerts** is bombed and the Proms re-locate to the Royal Albert Hall.

1942:

Vera Lynn records **The White Cliffs of Dover** with Mantovani at Decca Records and from America, Bing Crosby's White Christmas is a 'hit' together with Glenn Miller's **Moonlight Cocktail** and **Chattanooga Choo Choo.**

Serge Koussevitzky, Russian composer and music director, commissions Benjamin Britten to compose an opera, **Peter Grimes**.

Enid Blyton publishes **Five on a Treasure Island,** the first book of her **The Famous Five** Series.

1943:

In April the Ministry of Information release a film **Desert Victory** which goes on to win this year's Academy Award for Best Documentary Feature.

Three pigeons, 'White Vision', 'Winkie' and 'Tyke' become the first recipients of the **Dickin Medal,** an award for any animal displaying conspicuous gallantry and devotion to duty whilst serving with the armed forces or civil emergency forces.

1944:

The prohibition of married women working as teachers is lifted.

Laurence Olivier's **Henry V** is released. It is the first of Shakespeare's works to be filmed in colour.

A Child of Our Time by Michael Tippett has its first performances at the Adelphi Theatre.

Bing Crosby was 'big' in Britain and his **Swinging on a Star** from the film, **Going My Way** won the Oscar for best original song.

On the BBC wireless, **Much Binding in the Marsh** and **Variety Bandbox** make their debut.

1945:
The **BBC Light Programme** is launched, concentrating on broadcasting mainstream light music and entertainment.
Giles first appears in the Sunday Express; George Orwell's **Animal Farm** is published and Noël Coward's film **Brief Encounter** starring Celia Johnson and Trevor Howard is released.
The first of the **Poldark** novels by Winston Graham is published, **Ross Poldark**.

1946:
The American dance craze, the **Jitterbug** invades Britain.
The Royal Opera House in Covent Garden re-opens after the War with the Royal Ballet performing **The Sleeping Beauty**.
BBC radio debuts include **American Letter** by Alistair Cooke, **Woman's Hour** and **Dick Barton Special Agent**. BBC television is resumed.
The first post-war **FA Cup Final** is held at Wembley and Derby County beat Charlton Athletic.

1947:
Ealing Studios release their first Ealing Comedy, **Hue and Cry**.
Compton Mackenzie's comic novel **Whisky Galore** is published.
The first soft **toilet paper** goes on sale in the UK, at Harrods.
Conductor Malcolm Sargent is knighted for his services to music and Lizbeth Webb has a hit with **This is My Lovely Day** from the film **Bless the Bride**.

1948:
BBC radio debuts include **Take it From Here** and **Any Questions?**
The first open-air museum in Britain, the **Welsh Folk Museum** opens at St Fagans.
The first new comprehensive schools open in Potters Bar and Hillingdon.
The **'Black Widow'** road safety poster – 'Keep death off the road, Carelessness kills' is issued.

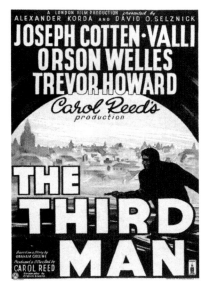

1949:
Book at Bedtime debuts on BBC radio,
Laurence Olivier's film **Hamlet** becomes the first British film to win an Oscar for 'Best Picture' and **The Third Man** is released.
Nineteen Eighty-Four by George Orwell is published and Enid Blyton introduces Noddy in **Little Noddy Goes to Toyland** and **The Secret Seven**.

SCIENCE

A Decade of Inventions

In the 1940s, research for and by the military played a significant part in all new developments. The atom bomb has influenced the world ever since, but there were many other inventions in the 1940s as well. Antibiotic penicillin; the insecticide DDT; synthetic rubber; kidney dialyses machines; the Jeep; Tupperware and duct tape. New technologies included radar, the jet engine, the Colossus electronic computer, and the first commercial flights with pressurised cabins were inaugurated.

The Aerosol Can

The concept of an aerosol originated as early as 1790 in France and in 1837 a soda siphon incorporating a valve was invented.

Metal spray cans were tested as early as 1862 but constructed from heavy steel they were too bulky to be commercially successful. In 1927, a Norwegian engineer patented the first aerosol can and valve that could hold and dispense products and propellant systems.

However, it was during the war that the US government funded research into a portable way for servicemen to spray malaria-carrying bugs and two department of Agriculture researchers developed a small aerosol can pressurised by a liquefied fluorocarbon.

America also developed a lightweight aluminium can, making a cheap and practical way to dispense hair spray, foams, powders and creams and when spray paint was invented in 1949, provided graffiti artists with the tools of their trade.

Velcro

Although Velcro was not released to the world until 1955, it all started in 1941 when George de Mestral, a Swiss inventor, took his dog for a walk in the woods. When he got home, he noticed that burrs from the burdock plant had attached themselves to the dog's fur and to his trousers.

Being a curious man, he examined the burrs under a microscope and saw that the tips of the burr contained tiny hooks that attached themselves to the fibres in his trousers. He spent the next 14 years trying to duplicate this system of 'hook and eye' fastener.

Velcro® Brand

1/2" WIDE
Velcro® Brand Tape Strips - Hook, Black
Strong acrylic adhesive can be used outdoors/indoor

Made of heat-treated nylon, with 300 hooks per square inch, Velcro is now found everywhere, blood pressure cuffs, orthopaedic devices, clothing and footwear, sporting and camping equipment, toys and recreation, airline seat cushions and Velcro was used in the first human artificial heart transplant to hold parts together.

Duct Tape

During the war, cartridges used for grenade launchers came boxed, sealed with wax and taped over to protect them from moisture. American soldiers needed to spend precious minutes, in the heat of battle, to open them.

Vesta Stoudt was working in a factory packing these cartridges and thought there must be an easier way. She came up with the idea of a tape made from strong, water-proof fabric. Her company not being interested, she wrote directly to the President who luckily passed on her proposal to the military.

Johnson & Johnson was assigned to develop the tape which now comprises a piece of mesh cloth and a pressure-sensitive adhesive. The original green sticky cloth became known as 'duck tape' to the troops and now, is used to make repairs from boots to furniture, in motorsports to patch up dents, by film crews who have a version called gaffer's tape, and even astronauts pack a roll when they go into space.

M&Ms

'The milk chocolate melts in your mouth, not in your hand' and the origins of M&Ms date back to the 1930s.

During the Spanish Civil War, American candy manufacturer, Forrest Mars, saw British soldiers eating Smarties - the sugar-coated chocolate beans that Rowntrees had begun making in 1882.

The sweets were popular with soldiers because they were less messy than pure chocolate. Forest Mars patented M&Ms in 1941, originally in cardboard tubes, but by 1948 the packaging changed to a plastic pouch.

LPs

In 1948, Columbia Records held a press conference at the Waldorf-Astoria Hotel in New York City to unveil their new technology, which was a non-breakable, 12-inch, microgroove disc that had a playing time of twenty-three minutes per side. Six times as much music as previous records and the start of the modern recording industry.

1950:

Feb: Clement Attlee wins the General Election for Labour giving them a 2nd term in government after their triumph in 1945.

Aug: 4,000 British troops are sent to Korea.

1951:

May: 3 George VI opens the Festival of Britain in London, including the Royal Festival Hall, Dome of Discovery and Skylon.

Oct: The Conservative Party led by Winston Churchill wins the General Election. It is six years since he was previously Prime Minister.

1952:

Feb: King George VI dies at Sandringham House, aged 56. He is succeeded by his daughter, Princess Elizabeth.

Dec: 4–9 The Great Smog blankets London, causing transport chaos and, it is believed, around 4,000 deaths.

1953:

Jan: Dwight D Eisenhower is sworn in as the 34th President of the United States.

Jan: Devastating North Sea Floods.

Jun: The coronation of Queen Elizabeth II takes place at Westminster Abbey. A public holiday is declared.

1954:

May: Roger Bannister becomes the first person to break the four-minute-mile at Oxford

Jul: Nearly a decade after the end of WW2, food rationing in the UK ends, with the lifting of restrictions on sale and purchase of meat.

1952: In February, compulsory Identity Cards are abolished. Brought in under the National Registration Act of 1939, every person, including children, had to carry it at all times, to show who they were and where they lived.

MOUNT EVEREST 1952

1953: On 29th May: Emund Hillary and Tenzing Norgay become the first men to reach the summit of Mount Everest. The British Expedition was led by Col. John Hunt and the news reached England on Coronation Day.

1955:

Apr: Winston Churchill resigns as Prime Minister due to ill-health and the Foreign Secretary, Anthony Eden, succeeds him.

Sep: ITV broadcasts the UK's first commercial television ending the BBC's 18-year monopoly. The first advertisement shown is for Gibbs SR toothpaste.

1956:

Feb: British spies, Guy Burgess and Donald Maclean show up in the Soviet Union after being missing for 5 years.

Apr: British MI6 diver Lionel Crabb, dives into Portsmouth Harbour to investigate a visiting Soviet cruiser and vanishes.

Jul: Gamal Abdel Nasser, the Egyptian leader, announces the nationalisation of the Suez Canal, beginning the Suez Crisis.

1957:

Jan: Anthony Eden resigns as Prime Minister due to ill health and Harold Macmillan succeeds him.

Mar: Egypt re-opens the Suez Canal and petrol rationing ends in May.

Jun: ERNIE selects the first Premium Bond winners.

1958:

Feb: The Manchester United FC team plane crashes at Munich Airport. 7 of the players are killed and an 8th dies later in hospital.

Jun: The Queen officially reopens Gatwick Airport which has been expanded at a cost of more than £7,000,000.

1959:

Jun: Christopher Cockerell's 'Hovercraft' is officially launched

Jul: UK Postcodes are introduced for the first time, in Norwich.

1956 Oct: The Queen switched on the world's first nuclear powered electricity generating station at Calder Hall, Cumberland. It was a fantastic engineering achievement, built within three years of cutting the first sod on the south side of the river Calder.

1958: In June, the first parking meter in Britain was installed in Grosvenor Square, near the US Embassy in Westminster. Parking for one hour cost six shillings (30p) and those who overstayed or neglected to pay at all received a £2 penalty.

THE HOME

During the early 50's, very few people had a television and the wireless reigned supreme. Daytime programmes were for wives, mothers and their children. 'Workers Playtime' continued to "come to you from a factory somewhere in England" and singers were interspersed with the major comedians of the day, Arthur Askey, Tommy Trinder, Charlie Chester and Ted Ray.

Music was important, with 'Music while you work' and 'Housewives Choice'. Soap operas gripped us, 'Mrs Dale's Diary' and 'The Archers'. Sunday lunchtimes meant 'Two-Way Family Favourites', music and messages for the troops in Germany. In the evening we could "Stop the roar of London's mighty traffic" and listen to 'In Town Tonight', and the children weren't forgotten, they had 'Listen with Mother', Children's Hour 'Children's Favourites' with Uncle Mac.

In 1958, Rowntree brought out their television advertisement, "Don't Forget the Fruit Gums Mum"

A tube of Rowntree's Fruit Gums lasts right round the clock!

Sweets were rationed until 1953 but children with a few pennies pocket money could choose sweeties from the rows of jars on the shelves. Four blackjacks or fruit salads for a penny, a Barratt's Sherbet Fountain with a stick of liquorice in it, raspberry drops, dolly mixture or toffees. You could 'smoke' a sweet cigarette whilst reading Dan Dare's adventures in Eagle or laugh with Radio Fun, Beano and Dandy comics.

IN THE 1950s

The drabness of the war years gave way by the mid '50s to an age of colour and plastic in the home. Textile restrictions had been lifted and consumers were eager for new brightly patterned curtains and upholstery, but it was the kitchen that was changed most, with the introductionsof coloured plastic goods.

The concept of 'built in' wall units and cupboards, rather than free standing wooden units appeared but it was only when stores such as MFI appeared that fitted kitchens become affordable for most.

In 1952 the nuclear family was the norm, father out at work and mother busy with the housework. Less than 10% of households had a refrigerator, meat was stored in a wire mesh 'safe' in the larder, vegetables wilted on a rack and shopping was done daily. It was the time of spam fritters, salmon sandwiches, tinned fruit with evaporated milk and ham salad for high tea on Sundays. Salad in the summer consisted of round lettuce, cucumber and tomatoes, and the only dressing available was Heinz Salad Cream, olive oil only came in tiny bottles from the chemist for your ears!

Many housewifes wanted a Kenwood Chef to make baking and food preparation easier. And these new domestic inventions coincided with an upsurge in 'do-it-yourself' or DIY from the mid-1950s. The nation that had adopted a 'make do and mend' attitude during wartime privations took very readily to the idea of improving their homes themselves.

1950 'Painting by numbers' kits are first marketed by the Palmer Show Card Paint Company in Detroit.

The Festival Ballet, founded by Alicia Markova and Anton Dolin makes its debut performance.

1951 Dennis the Menace makes his first appearance in The Beano comic.

The first ever Miss World beauty pageant is held as part of the Festival of Britain.

1952 The first TV detector van begins clamping down on the estimated 150,000 British households that watch television without a licence.

Vladimir Tretchikoff paints his best-selling work, 'Chinese Girl' sometimes known as 'The Green Lady'

'The Mousetrap' by Agatha Christie opens at the New Ambassadors Theatre.

1953 The current affairs series Panorama is first shown on BBC.

The 'Piltdown Man' is exposed as a hoax.

'The Moka', the first Italian espresso coffee bar is the first to open in London and Laura Ashley sells her first printed fabrics.

1954 Two months after the author's death, Richard Burton makes famous his 'First Voice' in Dylan Thomas's radio play, 'Under Milk Wood'.

'The Fellowship of the Ring', the first of three volumes of J.R.R. Tolkien's epic fantasy novel, 'The Lord of the Rings' is published.

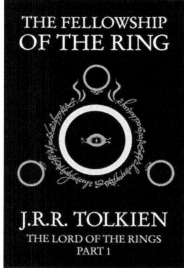

1955 Pietro Annigoni's iconic portrait of the Queen is unveiled.

The 'Guinness Book of Records' is first published.

1956 Harold Macmillan, Chancellor of the Exchequer, announces the launch of Premium Bonds with a top prize of £1,000.

The Queen awards Ninette de Valois's ballet school and companies the title "Royal" and they become the Royal Ballet of England.

1957 The cartoon character, Andy Capp first appears in northern editions of the 'Daily Mirror'.

The Queen broadcasts her first Royal Christmas Message on television.

1958 The first Duke of Edinburgh Award is presented at Buckingham Palace.

The practice of presenting debutantes to the royal court is abolished.

Both 'Grandstand' and 'Blue Peter' make their debut on BBC television.

1959 The ballerina, Margot Fonteyn is released from prison in Panama, having been suspected of being involved in a coup against the government.

BBC airs 'Juke Box Jury' chaired by David Jacobs, for the first time.

IN THE 1950s

SHE SAT DOWN ON A LITTLE BOULDER AND THEN BERTIE GOT 'A LITTLE BOLDER' TOO

1954, Donald McGill, the English graphic artist who painted and popularised 'saucy seaside postcards' was found guilty in Lincoln, of breaching the Obscene Publications Act of 1857. He was fined £50 with £25 costs.

The scenes he painted were most often at the seaside and featured an array of buxom young women, fat old ladies, drunken men, honeymoon couples and vicars, all displaying a fine level of social commentary and a 'naughty' sense of humour.

"I'm in a ticklish position here!"

FESTIVAL OF BRITAIN
1951

In 1951, the government took inspiration from the Great Exhibition of 1851, to organise the 'Festival of Britain' with the aim of promoting a feeling of recovery in the still war damaged country. Sited on the South Bank in London, the exhibits were to celebrate British industry, arts and science and led by a young architect, Hugh Casson, the buildings themselves turned out to be just as important and inspiring.

- The largest dome in the world at the time, standing 93ft tall with a diameter of 365ft which held exhibitions on the theme of discovery, the New World, the Polar regions, the Sea, the Sky and Outer Space.
- Adjacent to the Dome was the Skylon, a stunning, futuristic-looking structure, it was a vertical cigar shaped tower supported by cables that gave it the impression of floating above the ground.
- The Telekinema was a 400-seat, state-of-the-art, cinema which had the necessary technology to screen both films and large screen television and proved to be one of the most popular attractions.

Also built were the Royal Festival Hall and a new wing of the Science Museum whilst upriver from the main site was Battersea Park, home to the Festival fun-fair, pleasure gardens, rides and open-air amusements.

1950   The black and white film, **All the King's Men** picked up the Oscar for Best Picture of the year. Based on the Pulitzer Prize winning book by Robert Penn Warren, it relates the rise and fall of an ambitious and ruthless politician, Willie Stark, during the depression in the American South.

1951   **All About Eve** starred Bette Davis and Anne Baxter and received a record 14 Academy Award nominations – four of them for the female acting - and won six, including Best Picture. It also featured Marilyn Monroe in one of her earliest roles

1952   Gene Kelly and Leslie Caron in her acting debut, had a huge success with **An American in Paris**. The climax of the film is a 17-minute ballet danced by the pair causing controversy over part of Caron's dance sequence with a chair. The censor called it 'sexually provocative' to which, surprised, Caron answered, *"What can you do with a chair?"*

1953   **The Greatest Show on Earth** set in the Ringling Bros. and Barnum and Bailey Circus was certainly a great show. The circus troupe, 1,400 people appear, plus hundreds of animals and 60 railroad cars of equipment and tents. The actors learned their respective circus roles and participated in the acts.

1954   This year, the trials and tribulations of three US Army soldiers and their women in Hawaii during the lead up to the attack on Pearl Harbour won **From Here to Eternity** the accolades.

1955   **The Seven Year Itch** premièred and contains the famous image of Marilyn Monroe standing on a subway grate as her white dress is blown upwards by a passing train. **On the Waterfront** won the Oscar.

1956   The first and only entirely British film to have won the Oscar for Best Picture by this time was **Hamlet** starring Laurence Oliver in 1948 and the prize was not picked up again until **Tom Jones** in 1963.
An American romantic drama **Marty** was this year's winner and enjoyed international success, winning the Palme d'Or also.

1957   **Around the World in 80 days** was the first film to win Best Picture when all its fellow nominees were also filmed in colour.

1958   British director, David Lean's epic war film **The Bridge on the River Kwai** won the Academy Award for Best Picture. British actor Alec Guinness starred, and it became the highest earning film of the year.

1959   Leslie Caron was **Gigi** and the film won all nine of its Oscar nominations. The screenplay, songs and lyrics were written by Alan Jay Lerner and music by Frederick Loewe was arranged by André Previn.

British Film in the 1950s

If the 1940s was seen by many as 'the golden age' of British cinema, it was followed in the 50's by 'the dark age'. The two major cinema chains, Rank and Associated British Pictures embarked on a programme of cinema closures and admissions dropped by 500m over the ten years.

Even though no Oscars were won, there were good films: The most popular genre was the British war film. **The Cruel Sea, The Dam Busters, Reach for the Sky** and **Sink the Bismarck!** were top box-office attractions, while **The Bridge on the River Kwai** was the British cinema's biggest international success of the decade.

Some criticised the nostalgia but there were some changes to the traditional formula of male, stiff upper lip heroics, **A Town Like Alice** was shown from the female point of view and **Ice Cold in Alex** has an assertive female lead, the nurse who sorely tempts the neurotic British officer 'hero'..

Comedy was always popular. Ealing Studios produced **The Lavender Hill Mob**, **The Man in the White Suit** and **The Ladykillers** all featuring Britain's finest actor-star of the time, Alec Guinness. When Ealing closed in 1958, their gentle comedy was replaced by the raunchy high spirits of the **Carry On** films, peaking with **Carry On Nurse**.

The **St Trinian's** films had their following, as did the **Doctor** series, launched with spectacular success by **Doctor in the House**. **I'm All Right Jack** was a satire on industrial relations and **The Curse of Frankenstein** was famously described by the critic for the Observer newspaper as being amongst the most repulsive films she had ever seen. Quite a contrast to **Genevieve** and the London to Brighton car race.

At the end of the 50s, **Room at the Top** was a huge international success, and its sexual frankness and Northern realism ushered in a new era.

FASHION

AFTER THE WAR
THE 'NEW LOOK'

As the decade began, the simple, drab, styles from wartime remained as materials were still in short supply and for many this remained the case for several years. However, with the introduction of colour into the country again, in the home and in textiles, fashion for many women returned with a vengeance. The years are known for two silhouettes, that of Christian Dior's 'New Look', the tiny waist, pointy breasts and a full skirt to just below the knee, all achieved with a "waspie" girdle and the pointiest bra seen in history and the pencil slim tubular skirt, also placing emphasis on a narrow waist.

Neat, tailored suits with pencil skirts or fitted dresses, now updated with block colours were the choice for work and by the second half of the decade, the wide circle skirts in colourful cotton prints were in and were worn supported by bouffant net petticoats, stiffened either with conventional starch or a strong sugar solution, to give the right look.

THE *Lift* THAT NEVER LETS YOU DOWN

Elizabeth Taylor

ALL CHANGE

If a lady was 'formally dressed', she would wear short white cotton gloves for daytime and a decorative hat as a finishing touch. Hairstyles 'for the lady' were stiff, structured and arranged even when worn loose. The permanent wave, in styles worn by the Queen and Elizabeth Taylor, were universally worn, the styling more easily copied with the introduction of hair lacquers and plastic rollers. By 1955 almost 30,000 hair salons had sprung up in Britain.

Grace Kelly epitomised the elegance of the 50s, but there were many who rebelled against the look, including actress Audrey Hepburn who often wore simple black sweaters, flat shoes and short. They gave a continental, chic alternative and had many followers. In 1954, Chanel began to produce boxy classic Chanel suit jackets and slim skirts in braid trimmed, highly textured tweeds. The lines were straight down, losing the nipped in waist and this fashion was easy to copy by major chain stores and very wearable.

IN THE 1950s

THE YOUNG ONES

It was different, the new 'teenager' had their own ideas, girls sported youthful ponytails and were no longer prepared to look like their mothers until they were of age.

The consumer boom arrived with 'teen' clothes becoming available and fashion was influenced by America. Rock 'n' roll idols and film stars set fashions and many boys wanted the black leather and denim jeans look from Brando whilst girls embraced the 'preppie' full dirndl skirts teamed with a scoop neck blouse, back to front cardigan or tight polo neck.

There were the Teddy Boys and Beatniks, but the majority of British male teenagers looked smart. A basic blazer or jacket, with a fashionable narrow tie and even suede shoes.

WEDDING DRESS OF THE DECADE

Grace Kelly and Prince Rainier of Monaco married in 1956. Her dress was designed by Helen Rose, an American who spent the bulk of her career with MGM and was a wedding present from the film studio. It was made from 25 yards of silk taffeta and used antique rose-point lace and pearls.

The fitted bodice was overlaid with lace to the throat, culminating in a small standing collar and closed with a long centre row of tiny buttons. The long sleeves were also lace, and the dress had a full skirt and sweeping train.

The romantic look was completed by the lace and pearl encrusted prayer book the bride carried down the aisle.

WINNING THE POOLS

Football Pools were a 'betting pool' for predicting the outcome of top-level football matches taking place in the coming week. It was typically cheap to play and entries were sent to Littlewoods or Vernons, by post, or collected from your home by agents.

The most popular game was the Treble Chance where you had to predict the matches to end in a 'draw'.

O TWO RESULTS FROM EACH RULED SECTION				
180-1 TEN RESULTS				
South'pton	Bury			
Peterboro'	Barnsley			
Aldershot	Southport			
Bradford C.	Barrow			
Brentford	Mansfield			
Crewe Al.	Gillingham			
York C.	Doncaster			
Dunf'mline	Raith R.			
Dundee	Dundee U.			
Rangers	Hibernian			
Bolton W.	Fulham			
Everton	Sheff. W.			
Leicester	Notts F.			
Chelsea	Charlton			
Brighton	Hull City			
Colchester	Coventry			
Millwall	Watford			
Chesterf'ld	Exeter C.			
Oxford U.	Hartlepools			
Torquay U.	Lincoln C.			
Arsenal	Man. Un.			
Birmingh'm	Leyton O.			
Blackburn	Liverpool			
Blackpool	Wolves			
Man. City	Aston Villa			
Luton T.	Rotherham			
Middlesbro'	Huddersf'd			
Newcastle	Portsmouth			
Walsall	Preston			

CORRECT SCOR
DOUBLES · TREBLES · ACCUMULATI

Home	Away	H	A	H	A	H	A
Sheff. Un.	Ipswich T.						
Grimsby T.	Scunthorpe						
Leeds U.	Sunderland						
Swansea	Stoke C.						
Bristol R.	Crystal P.						
Notts C.	Bournem'th						

Max.: Doubles £1, Trebles & Accums. 5/-. Min. 3d.

SHORT LIST
11-1 THREE HOMES 12-1 THREE AWAYS

W. Brom.	Burnley
West Ham	Tottenh'm
Derby Co.	Cardiff C
Leeds Un.	Sunderl'd
Notts Co.	Bourne'th
Shrewsb'y	Bristol C
Airdrie	Kilmarn'k
Falkirk	Motherw'l

STAKES

TREBLE
12-1 THREE WINS 20-1 TWO WINS ONE DRAW

W. Brom.	Burnley
Notts Co.	Bourne'th
Shrewsb'y	Bristol C

Britain was almost obsessed with all things American after the war and the first Wimpy Bars opened in Britain in 1954, selling hamburgers, expresso coffee and milkshakes. Named after a fat friend of 'Popeye', the Wimpy bar added the 'British' elements of waitress service and cutlery. They became very popular, especially with the decade's 'new' teenagers who welcomed the addition to the high street's coffee bars and juke boxes.

CAN YOU COME OUT TO PLAY?

Friends would knock on the door straight after breakfast and you would often not come back till tea-time. Streets had little traffic and could be transformed with a couple of pullovers into a football or cricket pitch.

Towns had areas still devastated by bomb damage providing excellent dens and in the country, you could 'go up the woods', ideal for Cowboys and Indians. Those with bikes would cycle for miles, heading for the countryside or city parks to find trees to climb and fall out of, knees always seemed to be grazed and muddy. There were streams to paddle in or fish for stickle backs.

Girls could spend hours skipping or playing hopscotch drawn on the path, whilst their 'babies' slept in the toy prams alongside. Boys playing British bulldog would be rushing past girls, their dresses tucked into the legs of their knickers, practicing handstands against a wall or cartwheels. Saturday night was bath night!

IN THE 1950s

BUTLIN'S HOLIDAY CAMP SKEGNESS
IT'S QUICKER BY RAIL

THE GREAT BRITISH SEASIDE HOLIDAY

The heyday of the great British seaside holiday was in the 1950s and particularly for those living in industrial towns where 'wakes weeks', when the whole factory would shut down and all workers took their annual two weeks holiday at the same time. Convoys of coaches would leave the grime behind, ferrying happy families to the seaside. Blackpool or Scarborough, Brighton or Margate.

The choice was to stay in a guest house or hotel, or for thousands, it was the excitement of a holiday camp such as Butlins or Pontins. Heaven for children, the many activities on offer included the swimming pool, cinema, fairground rides all 'inclusive', no extra charge. Three meals a day were included, served in the communal dining hall and 'Red Coats' at Butlins, or 'Blue Coats' at Pontins, organised daytime activities for both adults and children. Even a 'knobbly knees' and 'gkamourous granny' contests. For the evenings, there was the traditional entertainment, song and dance and comedy shows.

The British seaside resorts provided fun and respite from daily life for the masses, with amusement arcades, candyfloss stalls and seafood shacks selling cockles and whelks in paper cones. Cafes served fish and chips with white bread and butter, accompanied by mugs of tea. There were donkey rides on the sand, roundabouts, helter-skelters and dodgems. On the prom shops sold rock, postcards, buckets and spades and, whatever the weather, families in rented deck chairs sheltered behind windbreaks on the beach, watching the children build sandcastles, play ball and paddle in the sea.

Only the unpredictable British weather could spoil the fun.

1950   The UK singles chart did not exist before 1952 and a song's popularity was measured by the sales of sheet music. This year's top sellers ranged from **You're Breaking My Heart** by Vic Damone, through **Bewitched** by Doris Day to **Rudolph the Red Nosed Reindeer**, the Christmas 'no 1' from Bing Crosby.

1951   **I Taut I Saw a Puddy Tat** was sung by Mel Blanc who was 'the voice' of Tweety and Silvester in the US cartoons. It was the best seller for three weeks, sold over 2m copies and has been recorded by several artists since. Less of a novelty, was **Too Young** by Jimmy Young, who went on to DJ for Radio 2 for almost 30 years.

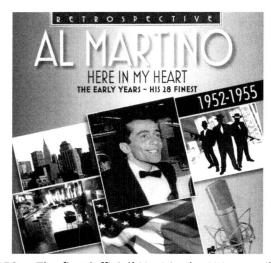

1952   The first 'official' No 1 in the UK, compiled from the best-selling songs by a telephone sample of about 20 shops and published in 'NME' in November was **Here in My Heart** by Al Martino.

1953   Frankie Lane was the singer of the year, **I Believe** topped the charts for 18 non-consecutive weeks and he had 8 top 10 entries, with 2 reaching No 1. Both David Whitfield and Frankie Lane reached a joint top spot, with the same song, at the same time **Answer Me.**

1954   **Secret Love** was Doris Day's second No1 and became the best-selling record of the year. Eddie Calvert, the British trumpeter had a No 1 for 9 weeks, with **Oh Mein Papa**.

1955   Songs seemed to stay at the top longer in the 50's, and Slim Whitmans **Rose Marie** from the musical of the same name, was there for 9 weeks. Tony Bennett made another song from a show, **Stranger in Paradise** from Kismet, a hit too. year but the best-seller was **I'll Be Home** by Pat Boone.

1956   Now, Rock 'n' Roll hit the world! Bill Hayley & his Comets, stormed to No 1 with **Rock Around the Clock** right at the beginning of the year but the best-seller was **I'll Be Home** by Pat Boone.

1957   This was a year for the Brits with hits from Tommy Steele **Singing the Blues**, Frankie Vaughan's **Garden of Eden**, Lonnie Donegan with **Cumberland Gap** and **Gamblin' Man** but the Canadian Paul Anka outsold them with **Diana**.

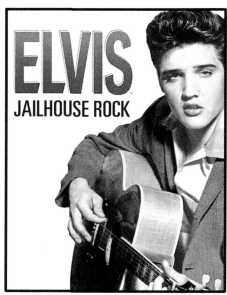

1958   Elvis Presley continued on his way to 21 UK No 1's with **Jailhouse Rock** and the Everly Brothers had the first of their No 1's with **All I Have to Do Is Dream.**

1959   **Living Doll** by Cliff Richard and the Drifters made it to No 1 and later with The Shadows with **Travelling Light.** Adam Faith makes his debut with **What Do You Want.**

IN THE 1950s

BUDDY HOLLY

During his short career, Holly wrote and recorded many songs. He is often regarded as the artist who defined the traditional rock-and-roll lineup of two guitars, bass, and drums.

That'll Be The Day topped the US "Best Sellers in Stores" chart in September 1957 when they also released **Peggy Sue.**

Buddy Holly (above) and Buddy Holly and the Crickets.(left)

The 50's legend had a huge posthumous hit with **It Doesn't Matter Anymore** and **Raining in My Heart** in 1959, shortly after he was tragically killed in a plane crash in the February. His death was the event later dubbed as "The Day the Music Died" by singer-songwriter Don McLean in his 1971 song **American Pie.**

BRITISH ROCK AND ROLL

In the '50s, American rock 'n' roll arrived in Britain, dominated the popular music world and became a huge influence on the newly burgeoning youth culture.

It was a fusion of rhythm and blues, gospel music, country and western and pop. Bill Hayley's '**Rock Around the Clock**', Elvis with '**Hound Dog**' and '**Jailhouse Rock**', Little Richard and Jerry Lee Lewis, inspired British the rock'n'roll groups who emerged from the already popular skiffle groups.

Tommy Steele was one of the first to become a teen idol, with Marty Wilde, Billy Fury and others soon following, but it was Cliff Richard and The Shadows' hit '**Move It**', in 1958, that caused British rock 'n' roll to explode.

Tommy Steele

Cliff Richards and The Shadows

Science and Nature

A Decade of Inventions

The 1950s was a period when a plethora of new innovations and inventions were made many still very much in use in the 21st Century. Credit cards, super glue, video tape recorder, oral contraceptives, non-stick Teflon pans, hovercraft, integrating circuit, microchip, transistor radio, heart pacemaker, wireless tv remote, solar panels, polio vaccine, automatic sliding doors, polypropylene, Fortran, the hard disk, power steering and of course, the hula hoop and Barbie dolls.

Black Box Flight Recorder

This invention by an Australian, David Warren, has saved many lives since it was introduced in 1953.

Before then, the cause of most plane crashes, unless there was a surviving pilot, remained unknown, and working as a researcher at an Aeronautical Laboratory in Melbourne, Warren realised that if there was a device in the cockpit that recorded the pilot's voice and read instruments, the information gathered could reveal the cause of the crash and could possibly prevent subsequent ones.

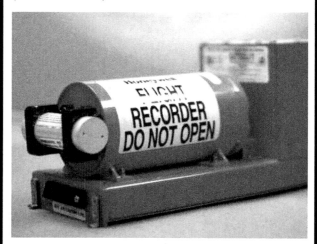

His first device called the Flight Memory Unit could record about four hours of voice and certain parameters but was rejected on grounds of privacy by the Australian aviation community.

Luckily, British officials accepted it, production of the devices in fireproof containers, began and it was taken up by airlines around the world. Some years later it was made compulsory for Australia.

Bar Codes

Joseph Woodland and Bernard Silver invented the first bar code in 1951. At the time Bernard was a graduate at Drexel Institute of Technology, Philadelphia which was contacted by a local food store that wanted a means to automatically read product information when customers checked out.

Woodland was at the beach thinking about this when he started drawing random lines in the sand with four of his fingers. He realised he had found one way to solve the food store owner's problem, data could be represented by varying the widths and spacings of parallel lines and thus be able to be read by a machine.

Using UV light sensitive ink he and his colleagues worked on prototypes until they came out with the scannable bar code which has helped make the modern economy.

IN THE 1950s

Winter of Terror

The Winter of Terror was a three-month period during the winter of 1950–1951 when the Alps were hit by the worst avalanche season ever seen. Thought to be the result of an Atlantic warm front meeting a polar cold front, the destruction mostly affected Austria and Switzerland.

A January snowstorm that lasted two days, added up to four metres of snowfall to a base that was already twice the seasonal average and strong winds caused drifting which led to unstable masses of snow being built up over wide areas. This was to come tumbling down in hundreds of avalanches, burying villages and killing in excess of 200 people.

Thousands of acres of valuable forest were damaged, livestock suffocated, and hundreds of buildings were destroyed. The Swiss town of Andermatt was hit by six avalanches within an hour and 13 people died.

Fifties Floods

1952: In August, the tiny village of Lynmouth, north Devon, suffered the worst river flood in English history. On the 15th, just over 9in (230mm) of rain fell, estimated at 90m tons, over north Devon and west Somerset.

The 1953 Floods in the Netherlands

1953: The great North Sea flood of January caused catastrophic damage and loss of life in Scotland, England, Belgium and The Netherlands and was Britain's worst peacetime disaster on record claiming the lives of 307 people.

In the Netherlands where 50% of the land is less than 1 metre (3.3 ft) above sea level there were 1,836 deaths and widespread damage

1950 The 4th **FIFA World Cup** is held for the first time since 1938 (1942 and 1946 were cancelled during the war). Brazil is the host nation and loses to Uruguay in the finals.

American Joey Maxim wins the light-heavyweight world **Boxing** title, stopping World Champion Freddie Mills of Britain in 10 rounds.

The 4th **British Empire Games** (later called the Commonwealth Games) are held in New Zealand.

1951 Ben Hogan wins the **Masters Tournament** for his 5th major title. He goes on to win the **US Open** title later in the year.

In **First Division football**, Tottenham Hotspur win the 1950/51 title and in the **FA Cup**, Newcastle United beats Blackpool.

1952 At the summer **Olympics** in Helsinki, Finland, Emil Zátopek of Czechoslovakia wins three gold medals. The 5,000m and 10,000m and the third - he decided at the last minute to compete in the first marathon of his life. He was nicknamed the 'Czech Locomotive'.

Rocky Marciano wins the **World Heavyweight Championship** title which he holds until 1956.

1953 Italian Alberto Ascari wins the **F1 Driver's Championship** for the second consecutive time, driving a Ferrari on both occasions.

Ken Rosewall won the **Australian Open** for his first grand slam title at just 18 years of age.

Maureen Connolly (USA) becomes the first woman to win the **Grand Slam** in tennis. The Australian Open, the French Open, Wimbledon and the US Open.

1954 At the **FIFA World Cup** held in Switzerland, Hungary squandered a 2-0 lead over West Germany to lose the final 3-2. Considered to be one of the most disappointing finals matches ever.

In **Athletics**, English runner Roger Bannister becames the first person in history to run one mile in under four minutes.

1955 In US thoroughbred **Horse Racing**, 'Nashua' beats 'Swaps' at Washington Park, 'Swaps' only loss in 9 starts. Nashua's owner-breeder, William Woodward Jr. dreams of owning a Derby winner but is shot dead by his wife before he can send 'Nashua' to England to train.

1956 Lew Hoad wins the **Australian Open** for his first grand slam title. He also wins the **French Open** and **Wimbledon** this year.

In **Cricket**, England off-spinner Jim Laker gains a world record taking 19 wickets in the Test match against Australia at Old Trafford. He takes a total of 46 wickets in the five Tests, a record in an England-Australia series.

1957 Jacques Anquetil of France wins the **Tour de France** for the first of his five times.

In **Football**, Stanley Matthews, 'The Wizard of the Dribble' and 'The Magician' makes his last appearance for England in the match against Denmark in Copenhagen.

1958 Pelé makes his debut at the **FIFA World Cup** in Sweden. Brazil defeats the host in the finals to win the cup.

The plane carrying the **Manchester United football team** crashes at Munich Airport, killing 44 people, including eight Manchester United players.

1959 Maria Bueno of Brazil won the **Wimbledon** Ladies Final at 19 years of age, her first grand slam title. She also won the **US Open** that year.

South African golfer, Gary Player, wins his first major title at **The Open** Championship.

The **Rugby** Five Nations Championship is won by France, the team's first outright championship title.

Swimming the English Channel

On 8th August 1950, Florence Chadwick, 'Queen of the Channel', set a new Women's record for swimming the 21 miles of the English Channel from France to England, in 13 hrs 20 mins.

Florence was a typist and swimming coach from California and achieved four successes in her ten attempts. In 1951 she became the first ever woman, at 32 years old, to swim from England to France, which also made her the first woman to ever swim the 'double'.

She made three England to France swims and each one took the record for the fastest time, going from 16 hrs 22 mins in 1951 to 13 hrs 55 mins in 1955. On her last three successful swims she also attempted to swim there-and-back but gave up on the return legs.

The first woman to ever swim the Channel was also an American, Gertrude Ederle, who in 1926, achieved a time of 14 hrs and 34 mins.

The first person to successfully cross the stretch of water was Captain Matthew Webb, who swam the distance in 1875 at his second attempt and took 21 hrs 45 mins.

Juan Manuel Fangio

In May 1950, the Formula One world championship era began, at Silverstone with Alfa Romeo becoming its first super-power, sweeping to victory at the start of the season and remaining unbeaten until the end. The Argentinian driver, a stocky, balding Argentine already in his 40s and nicknamed, 'El Chueco', the 'bowlegged or bandy legged one', dominated the first decade of Formula One, winning the World Driver's Championship five times. He raced for four different teams, Alfa Romeo, Ferrari, Mercedes-Benz and Maserati, winning 24 of his 52 F1 races, including his 'home' Grand Prix in Argentina four times.

At this time F1 cars were fast and physically demanding to drive, races were long and by the end of a GP, drivers often suffered blistered hands from the heavy steering and gear changing and their faces were sometimes covered in soot from the inboard brakes. In 1955, Fangio was teamed with a 25-year-old 'apprentice', Stirling Moss, Britain's brightest prospect.

By 1950, Britain was the world's biggest car exporter and most cars on our roads were built in Britain. Here are some of the famous cars.

Ford Popular

When launched in 1953, the Ford Popular was the cheapest car in Britain. But while robust and reliable, it was quite basic; even sun visors cost extra.

Vauxhall Cresta

While Vauxhall's Cresta brought a touch of chrome-clad American glamour to British roads in the 1950s these large cars often succumbed to rust. More than 300,000 were built in Luton from 1948 to 1965.

The Last Steam Trains

Great Britain was the first nation to use steam locomotives and Britain's railway is the oldest in the world but by 1955, a modernisation programme started to replace this vital cog of the nineteenth century industrial revolution with diesel and electric trains.

Morris Minor

More than 1.6 million of this design classic were manufactured and the Minor Series II and Minor 1000 belong to the 1950s.

The Mini

The Mini may be the greatest British classic car of all time. In 1959, Sir Alec Issigonis created a vehicle where passengers used 80% of its interior space. The Mini became an iconic, affordable, family car.

Jaguar XK140

A beautiful sports car with a sleek bonnet and sparkling wheels

In The 1950s

Britain's First Motorway

In December 1958, Prime Minister Harold Macmillan opened the Preston Bypass, the first ever section of motorway in Great Britain, planned as part of a larger scheme to build a north-south motorway network.

Nearly £3 million was spent on the construction of this original 8 ¼ mile, dual two lane, motorway after early work was hampered by foul weather and heavy rainfall which resulted in the postponement of various heavy engineering works. Ultimately, this meant the initial two-year plan was delayed by a further five months.

The following year, the first section of the M1 motorway was opened in November 1959 and with it, the first service station at Watford Gap. Initially there was no speed limit on the motorway and, over three lanes, it gave motorists the chance to drive 50 miles from St Albans to Rugby as fast as their car could manage. The design team anticipated that the road would cope with about 14,000 vehicles each day.

The De Havilland Comet

On 2nd May 1952, the Comet 1 airliner carried passengers on a scheduled commercial route for the very first time. The journey from London to Johannesburg was reportedly a sublimely smooth one. This new aircraft could carry 36 passengers, those in first class sat around tables, at a cruising speed of 450 mph – and a top speed of 503 mph - over a distance of 2,500 miles and BOAC's fleet was the envy of world airlines.

Despite the aim to provide affordable widespread travel in an age where air travel was still the preserve of the rich, the Comet attracted its fair share of highly esteemed passengers. Queen Elizabeth, Princess Margaret and the Queen Mother were all guests of Sir Geoffrey and Lady de Havilland on a special flight in June 1953 and became the first members of the Royal Family to fly by jet.

The advent of passenger jets transformed air travel. Between 1950 and 1960 the number of air passengers carried in the UK increased from just over one million to six million.

1960

May: Princess Margaret marries photographer, Anthony Armstrong-Jones at Westminster Abbey. It is the first royal marriage to be televised.

Nov: "Lady Chatterley's Lover" sells 200,000 copies in one day following its publication since the ban enforced in 1928 is lifted.

1961

Jan: The farthing, used since the 13th Century, ceases to be legal tender in the UK.

Apr: The US attack on "The Bay of Pigs" in Cuba was defeated within two days by Cuban forces under the direct command of their Premier, Fidel Castro.

1962

Jan: An outbreak of smallpox infects 45 and kills 19 in South Wales. 900,000 people in the region are vaccinated against the disease.

Dec: The "Big Freeze" starts in Britain. There are no frost-free nights until 5 March 1963.

1963

June: Kennedy: 'Ich bin ein Berliner' The US President Kennedy, has made a ground-breaking speech in Berlin offering American solidarity to the citizens of West Germany.

Aug: 'The Great Train Robbery' on the travelling Post Office train from Glasgow to Euston, takes place in Buckinghamshire.

1964

Mar: Radio Caroline, the 'pirate radio station' begins regular broadcasting from a ship just outside UK territorial waters off Felixstowe, Suffolk.

Oct: After thirteen years in power, the Conservatives are beaten by Labour at the General Election and Harold Wilson becomes Prime Minister.

The Tiller Girls At The London Palladium

1962: In April, the five-month-old strike by Equity, the actors' union, against the Independent television companies, ends, with actors gaining huge increases in basic pay rates.

1963: John F. Kennedy, the 35th president of the United States, was assassinated on November 22 in Dallas, Texas, while riding in a presidential motorcade. He was with his wife Jacqueline, Texas Governor John Connally, and Connally's wife Nellie when he was fatally shot from a nearby building by Lee Harvey Oswald. Governor Connally was seriously wounded in the attack. The motorcade rushed to the local hospital, where Kennedy was pronounced dead about 30 minutes after the shooting. Mr Connally recovered.

1969 APOLLO 11. Neil Armstrong becomes the first man to walk on the moon. "One small step for man, one giant leap for mankind."

1965: In January, Sir Winston Churchill dies aged 90. Sir Winston served as Prime Minister of the United Kingdom from 1940-45 and again from 1951-1955. He is best known for his wartime leadership as PM.

1965

Mar: 3,500 US Marines, the first American ground combat troops arrive in Da Nang, South Vietnam.

Aug: Elizabeth Lane is appointed as the first ever female High Court Judge. She is assigned to the Family Division.

1966

Jun: The first British credit card, the Barclaycard, is introduced by Barclays. It has a monopoly in the market until the Access Card is introduced in 1972.

Sept: HMS Resolution is launched at Barrow-in-Furness. It is the first of the Polaris ballistic missile submarines, armed with 16 Polaris A missiles.

1967

Jan: Donald Campbell, the racing driver and speedboat racer, was killed on Coniston Water whilst attempting to break his own speed record.

Dec: The Anglo-French Concorde supersonic aircraft was unveiled in Toulouse, France.

1968

Jun: The National Health Service reintroduces prescription charges, abolished by the Labour Govt. in 1965, at 2s 6d.

Sep: The General Post Office divides their single rate postal service into two. First-class letters at 5d and second-class at 4d.

1969

Mar: The Queen opens the Victoria Line on the London Underground. It is the first entirely new Underground line in London for 50 years.

Dec: The abolition of the death penalty for murder, having been suspended since 1965, was made permanent by Parliament.

At the beginning of the decade, the wireless was still the usual form of entertainment in the home and children could sit comfortably to "Listen with Mother" on the Light Programme and mother could carry on listening to "Woman's Hour" afterwards.

However, television was becoming increasingly affordable, and the two channels, BBC and ITV were joined in 1965 by BBC2. Dr Finlay's Casebook; The Black and White Minstrel Show; Top of the Pops; Perry Mason and Z Cars were the most popular shows of the 60's.

In 1962 the BBC bravely introduced a new satirical show, "That Was the Week That Was" which proved a big hit and by 1969, the BBC was converting programmes to colour.

Children's pocket money, probably 6d (2.5p) a week in the early years, could buy sweets. Black Jacks and Fruit Salads (4 for a penny (0.5p)), sweet cigarettes, lemonade crystals, gob stoppers, flying saucers or toffees, weighed by the shopkeeper in 2oz or 4oz paper bags. All could be eaten whilst reading a copy of The Beano or Dandy, Bunty or Jack and Jill comics.

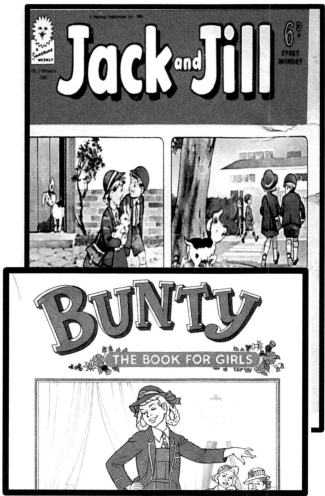

The simple, yet addictive party game Twister was introduced in 1966.

In the 60's the nuclear family was still the norm, father out at work and mother busy with the housework which was time consuming before the general possession of electrical labour-saving devices.

Washing up was done by hand and laundry gradually moved to machines over the decade.

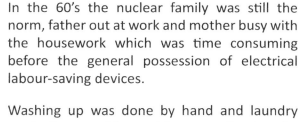

Twin tubs, one for washing and one for Spinning, became popular in the late 60's and were usually wheeled into the kitchen to be attached to the cold tap and afterwards, have the waste-water emptied into the sink. The 'housewife' had to be at home to transfer the wet washing from the washing tub to the spinning tub.

By the end of the 60's, 58% of households had a small refrigerator but no fridge/freezers, so shopping was still done regularly and, typically, meals were home cooked.

Chicken was expensive but beef was cheaper and olive oil came only in tiny bottles from the chemist to help clean your ears!

In Britain, the domestic freezer is still a luxury but by the mid 60's, some 700m fish fingers were among the 60,000 tons of frozen fish consumed with peas from 35,000 acres and 120,000 quick-frozen chickens.

I spy Birds Eye - the **freshest** VEGETABLES you can buy!

Goods came to you. The milkman delivered the milk to your doorstep, the baker brought the baskets of bread to the door, the greengrocer delivered and the 'pop man' came once a week with 'dandelion and burdock', 'cherryade' or 'cream soda' and the rag and bone man called down the street for your recycling.

ART AND CULTURE

1960 - 1963

1960 Frederick Ashton's 'La Fille Mal Gardée' premieres by The Royal Ballet at the Royal Opera House.
In court, Penguin Books who published 'Lady Chatterley's Lover' by DH Lawrence, is found not guilty of obscenity.

1961 The 'Betting & Gaming Act' comes into force which allows the operating of commercial Bingo halls.
'Ken' is introduced in the US as a boyfriend for 'Barbie'.

1962 Margot Fonteyn and Rudolf Nureyev first dance together in a Royal Ballet performance of Giselle, in London.
Dec John Steinbeck, American author is awarded the Nobel Prize in Literature. Aleksandr Solzhenitsyn's novella, "One Day in the Life of Ivan Denisovich" is published in Russia.

1963 The first Leeds Piano Competition is held, and Michael Roll is the winner.
Authors CS Lewis and Aldous Huxley both die on 23 November, but news of their deaths is overshadowed by the assassination of JFK.

Margot Fonteyn and Rudolf Nureyev performing The Sleeping Beauty.

Their partnership has been described as the greatest of all time.

1964 - 1969

1964 BBC television airs the first 'Top of the Pops'. Dusty Springfield is the very first artist to perform, with 'I Only Want to Be With You'.
Ernest Hemingway's memoirs of his years in Paris, 'A Moveable Feast' is published posthumously by his wife.

1965 Rembrandt's painting 'Titus' is sold at Christie's London fetching the then record price of 760,000 guineas. (£798,000).
The f*** word is spoken for the first time on television by Kenneth Tynan and two weeks later, Mary Whitehouse founds The National Viewers' and Listeners' Association.

1966 'Rosencrantz and Guildenstern Are Dead' by Tom Stoppard has its debut at the Edinburgh Festival Fringe.
BBC1 televises 'Cathy Come Home', a docudrama that is viewed by a quarter of the British public and goes on to influence attitudes to homelessness.

1967 **'The Summer of Love'.** Thousands of young 'flower children' descend on the west coast of America, for hippie music, hallucinogenic drugs, spiritual meditation and free-love.
BBC radio restructures. The Home Service becomes Radio 4, the Third Programme becomes Radio 3 and the Light Programme is split between Radio 1 (to compete with pirate radio) and Radio 2.

1968 The BBC repeat of the twenty-six episodes of 'The Forsyte Saga' on Sunday evening television, leads to reports of 'publicans and vicars complaining it was driving away their customers and worshippers, respectively' and of 'Evensong services being moved to avoid a clash'.

1969 The Beatles perform together for the last time on the rooftop of Apple Records in London. The impromptu concert was broken up by the police.

WOODSTOCK
MUSIC AND ARTS FAIR

JIMI HENDRIX   JANIS JOPLIN

♪ AUGUST 15-16-17 - 1969 ♪
THREE DAY PEACE AND MUSIC FESTIVAL

★ FRIDAY THE 15th - Joan Baez, Arlo Guthrie, Richie Havens, Sly & The Family Stone, Tim Hardin, Nick Benes, Sha Na Na

★ SATURDAY THE 16th - Canned Heat, Creedence Clearwater, Melanie, Grateful Dead, Janis Joplin Jefferson Airplane, Incredible String Band, Santana The Who, Paul Buttrfield, Keef Hartley

★ SUNDAY THE 17th - The Band, Crosby Stills Nash and Young, Ten Years After, Blood Sweat & Tears Joe Cocker, Jimi Hendrix, Mountain, Keef Hartley

AQUARIAN EXPOSITION
WHITE LAKE, NEW YORK

The three-day Woodstock Music Festival was held in August 1969 on a dairy farm in Bethel, New York. Nearly half a million young people arrived for "An Aquarian Experience: 3 Days of Peace and Music."
Now known simply as Woodstock, the festival was a huge success, but it did not go off without a hitch. The almost 500,000 people who turned up was unexpected and caused the organisers a headache which necessitated venue changes and this was before the bad weather, muddy conditions, lack of food and unsanitary conditions made life even more difficult.
Surprisingly, the event passed off peacefully, this fact attributed by most, to the amount of sex, psychedelic drugs and rock 'n roll that took place. Others say, couples were too busy 'making love not war' to cause trouble, either way, Woodstock earned its place in the halls of pop culture history fame.

"American artist Andy Warhol premieres his "Campbell's Soup Cans" exhibit in Los Angeles".

Andy Warhol famously borrowed familiar icons from everyday life and the media, among them celebrity and tabloid news photos, comic strips, and, in this work, the popular canned soup made by the Campbell's Soup Company. When he first exhibited "Campbell's Soup Cans", the images were displayed together on shelves, like products in a grocery aisle. At the time, Campbell's sold 32 soup varieties and each one of Warhol's 32 canvases corresponds to a different flavour, each having a different label. The first flavour, introduced in 1897, was tomato.
Each canvas was hand painted and the fleur de lys pattern round each can's bottom edge was hand stamped. Warhol said, "I used to drink Campbell's Soup. I used to have the same lunch every day, for 20 years, I guess!"

FILMS

1960 - 1963

1960   **Ben Hur**, the religious epic, was a remake of a 1925 silent film with a similar title and had the largest budget ($15.175m) and the largest sets built of any film produced at the time.

1961   Billy Wilder's risqué tragi-comedy **The Apartment** won the Academy Award for Best Picture. Starring Jack Lemmon and Shirley MacLaine, it tells a story of an ambitious, lonely insurance clerk who lends out his New York apartment to executives for their love affairs.

1962   New Films released this year included, **Lolita** starring James Mason and Sue Lyon. **Dr No**, the first James Bond film, starring Sean Connery and Ursula Andress and **What Ever Happened to Baby Jane?** a horror film with Bette Davis

1963   **Lawrence of Arabia,** based on author TS Eliot's book 'Seven Pillars of Wisdom' and starring Peter O'Toole and Alec Guinness won the Oscar for Best Picture.
The publicity of the affair between the stars, Elizabeth Taylor and Richard Burton, helped make **Cleopatra** a huge box office success but the enormous production costs, caused the film to be a financial disaster.

1964 - 1969

1964   The historical adventure, sex comedy romp **Tom Jones** won four Oscars, Best Picture, Best Director, Best Adapted Screenplay and Best Musical Score. Albert Finney starred as the titular hero and Susannah York as the girl he loves.

1965   Winning the Oscar this year, the film **My Fair Lady,** based on George Bernard Shaw's play 'Pygmalion', tells the story of Eliza Doolittle and her quest to 'speak proper' in order to be presentable in Edwardian London's high society. Rex Harrison and Audrey Hepburn starred and it became the 2nd highest grossing film of the year just behind **The Sound of Music** which won the Academy Award the following year.

1966   **The Good, the Bad and the Ugly** was directed by Sergio Leonie, the Italian director who gave rise to the term 'spaghetti western'- a genre of westerns produced and directed by Italians. Clint Eastwood was the Good, Lee Van Cleef, the Bad and Eli Wallach, the Ugly. The film was a huge success and catapulted Clint Eastwood to fame.

1967   The fun filled seduction of Benjamin Braddock by Mrs Robinson in **The Graduate** made the film the biggest grossing production of the year world-wide.

1968   The famous quote "They call me Mister Tibbs" comes from **In the Heat of the Night** where Sidney Poitier plays Virgil Tibbs, a black police detective from Philadelphia, caught up in a murder investigation in racially hostile Mississippi. Rod Steiger is the white chief of police.

1969   **Oliver** the musical based on Dicken's novel and Lionel Bart's stage show, carried off the Oscar for Best Picture.
Editor's Note: The Academy Awards are held in February and each year's awards are presented for films that were first shown during the full preceding calendar year from January 1 to December 31 Los Angelis, California. Source: Wikipedia

THE FIRST JAMES BOND FILM!

HARRY SALTZMAN and ALBERT R. BROCCOLI PRESENT

IAN FLEMING'S

Dr. NO

TECHNICOLOR

SEAN CONNERY AS 007 · URSULA ANDRESS · JOSEPH WISEMAN · JACK LOI

MAIBAUM HARWOOD MATHER YOUNG SALT,

This was the first-ever launch of a James Bond film in a cinema and was attended by the stars, Sean Connery and Ursula Andress together with the James Bond creator Ian Fleming. The plot of this British spy film revolves around James Bond who needs to solve the mystery of the strange disappearance of a British agent to Jamaica and finds an underground base belonging to Dr No who is plotting to disrupt the American space launch with a radio beam weapon. The film was condemned by The Vatican as "a dangerous mixture of violence, vulgarity, sadism, and sex".

1962 : "West Side Story" Wins The Academy Awards "Best Picture" category.

The musical with lyrics by Stephen Sondheim and music by Leonard Bernstein was inspired by the story of William Shakespeare's "Romeo and Juliet". Set in the mid 1950s in Upper West Side of New York City, which was then, a cosmopolitan working-class area, it follows the rivalry between the Jets and the Sharks, two teenage street gangs from different ethnic backgrounds.

The Sharks are from Puerto Rico and are taunted by the white Jets gang. The hero, Tony, a former member of the Jets falls in love with Maria, the sister of the leader of the Sharks. The sophisticated music and the extended dance scenes, focussing on the social problems marked a turning point in musical theatre. The film starred Natalie Wood and Richard Beymer.

FASHION

CHANGING FASHION

It was a decade of three parts for fashion. The first years were reminiscent of the fifties, conservative and restrained, classic in style and design. Jackie Kennedy, the President's glamorous wife, was very influential with her tailored suit dresses and pill box hats, white pearls and kitten heels.

The hairdresser was of extreme importance. Beehive coiffures worn by the likes of Dusty Springfield and Brigitte Bardot were imitated by women of all ages and Audrey Hepburn popularised the high bosom, sleeveless dress. Whilst low, square toed shoes were high fashion, 'on the street', stilettos rivalled them.

THE MODS

In the mid-60s, the look had become sleeker and more modern. The lines were form-fitting but didn't try to accentuate curves. There were brighter colours and for the young, the Mod style.

Male mods took on a smooth, sophisticated look that included tailor-made suits with narrow lapels, thin ties, button-down collar shirts and wool jumpers.

The pea coat and Chelsea boots looked very 'London'. The Beatles were leading the way, hair started to grow longer, and trousers lost the baggy, comfortable fit of the 1950's.

For girls, shift dresses and mini skirts became shorter and shorter, worn with flat shoes or 'go go boots', short hair with eyebrow brushing fringes, and little makeup, just a pale lipstick and false eyelashes.

Slender models like Jean Shrimpton and Twiggy exemplified the look and new, exciting designers emerged such as Mary Quant. Television shows like 'Ready Steady Go!' showed their audiences at home, what they should be wearing.

In The 1960s

The Hippies

For the young, jeans were becoming ubiquitous both for men and women, skin-tight drainpipes through to the flared bottoms of the late years. London had taken over from Paris to become the fashion centre of the world and in contrast to the beginning of the decade, the end was the exact opposite.

Bright, swirling colours. Psychedelic, tie-dye shirts, long hair and beards were commonplace. Individualism was the word and mini skirts were worn alongside brightly coloured and patterned tunics with flowing long skirts.

Carnaby Street

By 1967, Carnaby Street was popular with followers of the mod and hippie styles. Many fashion designers, such as Mary Quant, Lord John and Irvine Sellars, had premises there, and underground music bars, such as the Roaring Twenties, opened in the surrounding streets.

Bands such as the Small Faces, The Who and The Rolling Stones appeared in the area, to work at the legendary Marquee Club round the corner in Wardour Street, to shop, and to socialise. The Street became one of the coolest destinations associated with 1960s Swinging London.

THE PACKAGE HOLIDAY

By the mid-sixties, the traditional British seaside holiday, sandcastles, donkey rides, sticks of rock and fish and chips on the beach was gradually giving way to the new and exciting Package Holiday in the sun.

Tour operators began taking plane loads of holidaymakers abroad, almost exclusively to Europe and to Spain in particular. Hotels were springing up everywhere, often obscuring the 'exotic views' that the tourists were promised and were basic with rather simple local fare, which even then was not to the taste of a large majority. Restaurants flourished with 'Full English Breakfast' posters displayed all over the windows, tea and beer were in demand.

By the end of the decade, Luton Airport, a favourite with the tour firms, had flights arriving back every hour full of sunburnt Brits wearing sombreros and clutching Spanish donkeys and maracas.

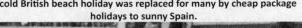

A cold British beach holiday was replaced for many by cheap package holidays to sunny Spain.

"LET'S GO FOR A CHINESE"

A 'Greasy Spoon'

A cheese-pineapple hedgehog

In the early 1960s, eating out was expensive and apart from 'greasy spoon' cafes, or a packet of salted crisps at a pub, dining out was limited to formal restaurants. However, with a rise in immigrants from Asia, Chinese and Indian restaurants were springing up and their relatively affordable and tasty food became so popular that Vesta brought out their first 'foreign convenience' foods, the Vesta Curries and Vesta Chow Mein.

A cheaper alternative was inviting friends to eat at home, and the dinner party boomed from the end of the decade. Pre-dinner drinks were often served with cubes of tinned pineapple and cheddar cheese on sticks, stuck into half a tinfoil covered grapefruit to look like a hedgehog – the height of 60s sophistication! The main course might feature the fashionable 'spaghetti bolognese', and 'Blue Nun', Mateus Rosé or Chianti wine, adding a hint of sophistication to the new 'smart' set's evening.

IN THE 1960s

2nd isle of wight festival of music 1969

Teenage Leisure

The 60's became the era for the teenager, but it started off with the same disciplines as the fifties. At school the teachers commanded respect and gave out punishment when it was not given. Parents could determine when and where their children could be out of house, gave sons and daughters chores to do and families ate together and watched television together.

Scouts and Guides were still very popular and a natural progression from the years as Cubs and Brownies and Outward Bounding or working for the Duke of Edinburgh Awards remained popular for many, but as the decade wore on, the lure of the new found freedom for the young was hard for many to overcome. Coffee bars became the place to meet, drink coffee or chocolate, listen to the latest hits on the juke box and talk with friends. The political climate influenced them, they demonstrated in the streets against the Vietnam War, for civil rights and to 'Ban the Bomb'. They developed the 'hippie' point of view, advocating non-violence and love, and by the end of the decade, "Make Love not War" was the 'flower children's' mantra.

Outdoor music festivals sprang up all over the country and thousands of, usually mud-caked, teenagers gathered to listen to their favourite artists, rock concerts played to packed houses and the young experimented with marijuana and LSD. Psychedelic art was incorporated into films, epitomised by the Beatles' 'Yellow Submarine'.

1960   **Poor Me by Adam Faith**, a teen idol, reached number 1 and stayed there for two weeks whilst his previous number 1 hit, **What Do You Want** was still in the top ten. The Everly Brothers, the American rock duo, had their fifth number 1 with **Cathy's Clown**. Their first was Bye Bye Love in 1957. A surprise number 1 for four weeks was by Lonnie Donnegan, the skiffle singer, with **My Old Man's a Dustman.**

1961   **Wooden Heart** sung by Elvis Presley stayed at number 1 for six weeks and became the best-selling UK single of the year. Johnny Leyton had a three-week number 1 with **Johnny Remember Me** in August and it returned to the number 1 spot again at the end of September. Teenage singer and actress Helen Shapiro, had her second number one, **Walkin' Back to Happiness**, whilst still only fifteen.

1962   The top selling single of the year was by the Australian singer, Frank Ifield. **I Remember You** was sung in a yodelling, country-music style.
Acker Bilk's **Stranger on the Shore** becomes the first British recording to reach the number 1 spot on the US Billboard Hot 100.
The Rolling Stones make their debut at London's Marquee Club, opening for Long John Baldry.

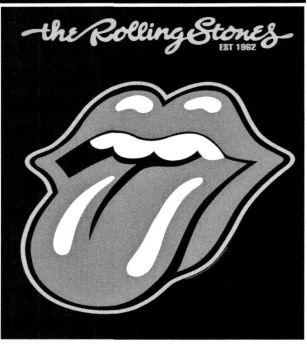

1962: The Rolling Stones make their debut at London's Marquee Club playing the rock n' roll of Chuck Berry and Bo Diddley.

1963   The Beatles have three number 1's in the UK charts in their first year. **From Me to You, She Loves You** and **I Want to Hold Your Hand.** Their debut album, **Please Please Me**, reaches the top of the album charts.
Produced by Phil Spector, The Crystals have a hit with **And Then He Kissed Me**
How Do You Do What You Do to Me, the debut single by Liverpudlian band Gerry and the Pacemakers, stays at number 1 for three weeks in April.

1964 The Hollies, the Merseybeat group founded by school friends Allan Clarke and Graham Nash, reach number 2 in the UK charts with **Just One Look**, a cover of the song by Doris Troy in the US.
Originally written by Burt Bacharach for Dionne Warwick, **Anyone Who Had a** Heart, sung by Cilla Black, became a UK number 1 for three weeks and was also the fourth best-selling single of 1964 in the UK, with sales of around 950,000 copies.

"The Fab Four", John Lennon, Paul McCartney, George Harrison and Ringo Star were the ultimate pop phenomenon of the '60s.

1965 Unchained Melody by The Righteous Brothers, with a solo by Bobby Hatfield becomes a jukebox standard. **Its Not Unusual** sung by Tom Jones becomes an international hit after being promoted by the offshore, pirate radio station, Radio Caroline. **Get Off of My Cloud** by The Rolling Stones was written by Mick Jagger and Keith Richards as a single to follow their previous hit of the year, **(I Can't Get No) Satisfaction**.

1966 Nancy Sinatra with **These Boots Are Made for Walkin'** reaches number 1.
Good Vibrations sung by The Beach Boys, becomes an immediate hit both sides of the Atlantic.
Ike and Tina Turner released **River Deep, Mountain High** and their popularity soars in the UK after a tour with The Rolling Stones.

1967 Waterloo Sunset by The Kinks, written by Ray Davies, reached number 2 in the British charts and was a top 10 hit in Australia, New Zealand and most of Europe. In North America, it failed to chart.
A Whiter Shade of Pale the debut single by Procul Harem stays at number 1 for eight weeks.
Sandie Shaw wins the Eurovision Song Contest with **Puppet on a String**.

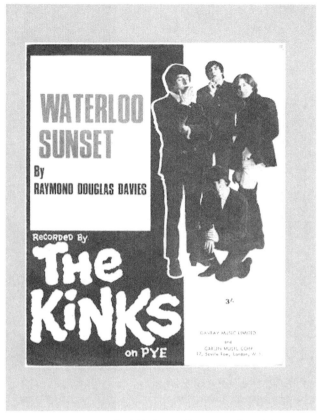

1968 Dusty Springfield's **Son of a Preacher Man** was her last top thirty hit until her collaboration with The Pet Shop Boys in 1987. In 1994, **Preacher Man** was included in Tarantino's film 'Pulp Fiction'.
Manfred Mann has a resounding success with **Mighty Quinn**, their third UK number 1 and third hit singing a song written by Bob Dylan.
The comedy group The Scaffold's record, **Lily the Pink** released in November became number 1 for the four weeks over the Christmas holidays.

1969 **Where Do You Go To (My Lovely)?** by the British singer-songwriter Peter Sarstedt stayed at number 1 for four weeks.
I Heard It Through the Grapevine was written in 1966 and recorded by Gladys Knight and the Pips. However, it was the version by Marvin Gaye that took the number 1 spot in the UK for three weeks and became the biggest hit single on the Motown label.
Je t'aime… moi non plus was written in 1967 for Brigitte Bardot but Serge Gainsbourg and Jane Birkin recorded the best known version and the duet reached number 1 in the UK. It was banned in several countries due to its overtly sexual content.

Science and Nature

The London Smog

Britain still experienced "pea-soupers" in the 60's and in December 1962, London suffered under a choking blanket of smog. After three days, the noxious layer spread all over the country.

Smog is a concentration of smoke particles and other substances such as sulphur dioxide, combined with fog in conditions of low temperature, high pressure and lack of wind. Visibility was reduced such that a light could only be seen at 50ft and in spite of people covering their faces with scarves, surgical masks or handkerchiefs, the overwhelming smell of sulphur and coal smoke left an unpleasant metallic taste in the mouth and irritated eyes and noses. Bronchitis increased significantly and it is estimated that, in Greater London alone, there were 700 deaths in total.

In 1962, the Duke of Edinburgh was in New York for the inaugural dinner of the US branch of the World Wildlife Fund, first set up in Zurich in 1961, and warned his audience that our descendants could be forced to live in a world where the only living creature would be man himself -"*always assuming,*" he said, "*that we don't destroy ourselves as well in the meantime.*"

In his speech, the Duke described poachers who were threatening extermination of many big game animals in Africa as "killers for profit … the get-rich-at-any-price mob." African poachers, he said, were killing off the rhinoceros to get its horn for export to China, "*where, for some incomprehensible reason, they seem to think it acts as an aphrodisiac.*" The Duke also criticised the status seekers – people "like the eagle chasers". The bald eagle in North America was being chased and killed by people in light aeroplanes who seem to think it smart to own its feathers and claws.

"*What is needed, above all now,*" he said, "*are people all over the world who understand the problem and really care about it. People who have the courage to see that the conservation laws are obeyed.*"

Duke of Edinburgh Launches World Wildlife Fund

Write-Protect Tab | Supply Reel | Slip Sheet | Take-up Reel
Guide Roller | Magnetic Shield | Pressure Pad | Capstan Hole

The Cassette Tape

The cassette tape was first developed by Philips in Belgium in 1962. These two small spools inside its plastic case, which wind magnetic-coated film on which the audio content is stored and pass it from one side to the other, meant music could now be recorded and shared by everyone.

Up until now, music was typically recorded on vinyl which needed a record player, or on reel-to-reel recorders which were comparatively expensive and difficult to use and neither of which were portable. The cassette player allowed individuals to record their favourite songs easily and also take their music with them "on-the-go". Music lovers soon learned how to create their own mixed tapes, for themselves or to share with friends.

More than 3 billion tapes were sold between 1962 and 1988.

The Aberfan Disaster

On 21 October 1966, the worst mining-related disaster in British history took place in Aberfan, in South Wales. Coal was mined there for domestic heating and the waste was dumped at the top of the valley on land of no economic value. But crucially, it was tipped on highly porous sandstone which overlaid at least one natural spring.

During October 1966 heavy rainfall led to a build-up of water within this tip and caused it to collapse. With a deafening roar, 107 cu m of black slurry turned into an avalanche. The deluge leapt over the old railway embankment into the village where destroyed 18 houses and Pant Glas Junior School together with part of the neighbouring County Secondary School.

In total, 144 lives were lost, 116 of them children, 109 of these were aged between seven and ten and died in their classrooms on the last day before half term. Of the 28 adults who died, five were primary school teachers.

The official inquiry placed the blame entirely on the National Coal Board.

SPORT

1960 - 1969

1960 In tennis, Rod Laver wins his first grand slam title as a 21-year-old taking the **Australian Open.**

Jack Brabham wins the **F1 driver's championship** for the second straight time.

1961 **Five Nations Championship** (now 6 Nations) rugby series is won by France.

Tottenham Hotspur beat Leicester City 2-0 in the **FA Cup Final**.

1962 Sonny Liston knocks out Floyd Pattison after two minutes into the first round of the "Boxing World Title" fight in Chicago.

1963 Mill House, at 18 hands, known as 'The Big Horse', wins the **Cheltenham Gold Cup.**

1964 The **Tour de France i**s won by Jacques Anquetil of France, the first cyclist to win the Tour five times. 1957 and 1961-64.

1965 At the **Masters** in Atlanta, Jack Nicklaus shoots a record 17 under par to win the tournament.

In the **FA Cup Final** at Wembley, Liverpool beats Leeds United 2-1.

1966 England defeat Germany to win the **FIFA World Cup**

1967 Defending champion Billie Jean King defeats Ann Haydon-Jones in the **Wimbledon Women's Singles Championship**.

The New York Yacht Club retains the **America's Cup** when 'Intrepid' beat the Australian challenger 'Dame Pattie', 4 races to 1.

1968 English International cricketer Basil D'Oliveira, of 'Cape Coloured' background, is excluded from the **MCC South African tour** side, leading to turmoil in the world of cricket.

1969 **The Grand National i**s won by 12-year-old Highland Wedding by 12 lengths.

1966 FIFA WORLD CUP

On July 30th, England and West Germany lined up at Wembley to determine the winner of the 'Jules Rimet Trophy', the prize for winning the World Cup. England won 4-2 after extra time and the match is remembered for Geoff Hurst's hat-trick and the controversial third goal awarded to England by the referee and linesman.

In addition to an attendance of 96,924 at the stadium, the British television audience peaked at 32.3 million viewers, making it the UK's most-watched television event ever.

It was the first occasion that England had hosted, or won, the World Cup and was to remain their only major tournament win. It was also the nation's last final at a major international football tournament for 55 years, until 2021 when England reached the Euro Final but lost to Italy after a penalty shootout.

IN THE 1960s

1964 OLYMPIC GAMES

In 1964, the first Olympic Games to be held in Asia, took place in Japan during October to avoid the city's midsummer heat and humidity and the September typhoon season. It marked many milestones in the history of the modern Games; a cinder running track was used for the last time in the athletics events, whilst a fibreglass pole was used for the first time in the pole-vaulting competition. These Games were also the last occasion that hand timing by stopwatch was used for official timing.

25 world records were broken and 52 of a possible 61 Olympic records were also broken. Ethiopian runner Abebe Bikila won his second consecutive Olympic marathon. Bob Hayes won the men's 100 metres and then anchored the US 400 metre relay team to a world record victory. Peter Snell, the New Zealand middle-distance runner, won both the 800 and 1500 metres, the only man to have done so in the same Olympics since 1920. Ann Packer of Britain made a record-breaking debut winning gold in the 800 metres and silver in the 400 metres.

Peter Snell, winning the 1500 metres.

CASSIUS CLAY HEAVYWEIGHT CHAMPION OF THE WORLD

In 1964, Cassius Clay, later this year to be known as Muhammad Ali, fought and gained Sonny Liston's title of Heavyweight Champion of the World. The big fight took place in Miami Beach in February.

Liston was an intimidating fighter and Clay was the 7-1 under-dog, but still he engaged in taunting his opponent during the build-up to the fight, dubbing him *"the big ugly bear"*, stating *"Liston even smells like a bear"* and claiming, *"After I beat him, I'm going to donate him to the zoo!"*
The result of the fight was a major upset as Clay's speed and mobility kept him out of trouble and in the third round hit Liston with a combination that opened a cut under his left eye and eventually, Liston could not come out for the seventh round.
A triumphant Clay rushed to the edge of the ring and, pointing to the ringside press, shouted: *"Eat your words!"* adding the words he was to live up to for the rest of his life, *"I am the greatest!"*

TRANSPORT

Trolleybuses were taken out of service in London in May having served since 1931.

How luxurious can an Austin Seven get?

The revolutionary Mini was the fastest selling small car in Britain in the 60s. Despite the promise of the adverts early models were slow and unreliable and although promoted as a luxury family car, it was uncomfortable and cramped.

THE VICKERS VC10

The 60's produced Britain's biggest airliner to date, the four jet Vickers VC10. With a towering tailplane, high as a four-storey house, the airliner weighed 150 tons fully loaded and was 158ft long. In service with BOAC and other airlines from the end of 1963 until 1981, the plane could carry 150 passengers at flew at 600mph over distances exceeding 4,000 miles. From 1965 they were also used as strategic air transports for the RAF.

CARS OF THE DECADE

The importance of personal transport increased dramatically during the Sixties and three of the images inextricably linked with the decade are the three-wheeler 'bubble car', the sleek, sexy, elongated E-type Jaguar and VW Camper Van.

MODS AND ROCKERS
SCOOTERS v MOTOR BIKES

Mods and Rockers were two rival British youth sub-cultures of the 1960's with a tendency to riot on Brighton beach.

They had very different outlooks: The Mods thought of themselves as sophisticated, stylish and in touch with the times. The motor cycling centred Rockers thought the Mods effeminate snobs!

They had very different appearances: Mods centred on fashion and wore suits or other clean-cut outfits. The Rockers wore black leather jackets and motorcycle boots or sometimes, 'brothel creeper' shoes.

They had very different tastes in music. The Mods favoured Soul and African American R&B. The Rockers went for Rock 'n Roll.

So not surprisingly, they had very different tastes in transport.

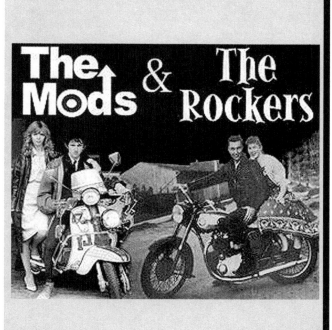

THE HOVERCRAFT

The great British invention of the decade was the Hovercraft. It was developed by Briton, Sir Christopher Cockerell. Saunders Roe, the flying boat firm at Cowes on the Isle of Wight built the prototype SR.N1, 20ft craft which first took to the seas in July 1959, crossing the English Channel from Calais to Dover in two hours with the inventor onboard. In 1961 hovercraft skirts were introduced to the design which provided far greater performance abilities and sea keeping.

The Hovercraft was a revolution in sea travel and the 1960's saw a fleet of craft crossing from the south coast to the Isle of Wight. They are now used throughout the world as specialised transports in disaster relief, coastguard, military and survey applications, as well as for sport or passenger service.

1970 - 1974

1970:
Jan: The age of majority for most legal purposes was reduced from 21 to 18 under terms of the Family Law Reform Act 1969.

Mar: Ian Smith declares Rhodesia a Republic and the British government refuses to recognise the new state.

1971:
Feb: Decimal Day. The UK and the Republic of Ireland both change to decimal currency.

Mar: The 'Daily Sketch', Britain's oldest tabloid newspaper is absorbed by the 'Daily Mail' after 62 years.

1972:
June: The 'Watergate' scandal begins in Richard Nixon's administration in the US.

Sep: The school leaving age in the UK was raised from 15 to 16 for pupils leaving at the end of the academic year.

1973:
Jan: The United Kingdom joins the European Economic Community, later to become the EU.

Sep: The IRA detonate bombs in Manchester and Victoria Station London and two days later, Oxford St. and Sloane Square.

1974:
Jan: Until March, the 3-day week is introduced by the Conservative Government to conserve electricity during the miners' strike.

Nov: 21 people are killed and 182 injured when the IRA set bombs in two Birmingham pubs.

1974: McDonald's open their first UK restaurant in South London. The traditional café was losing out, slow ordering and service with food served at tables was not as appealing as the clean, fast service and lower prices of this new fast food.

1974: In February, Harold Wilson becomes Prime Minister for the second time (first 1964-70) with a minority Government after Edward Heath resigns having failed to clinch a coalition with the Liberals. In the second general election of the year in October, Labour win with a majority of only 3 seats.

In June and July 1976, the UK experienced a heat wave. Temperatures peak at 35.9° and the whole country suffers a severe drought. Forest fires broke out, crops failed, and reservoirs dried up causing serious water shortages. The heatwave also produced swarms of ladybirds across the south and east.

On the 7th June,1977, more than one million people lined the streets of London to watch the Queen and Prince Phillip lead a procession in the golden state coach, to St Paul's at the start of a week of the Queen's Silver Jubilee celebrations – 25 years on the throne. People all over the country held street or village parties to celebrate, more than 100,000 cards were received by the Queen and 30,000 Jubilee medals were given out.

1975 - 1979

1975:
Feb: Margaret Thatcher defeats Edward Heath to become the first female leader of the Conservative Party.

Apr: The Vietnam War ends with the Fall of Saigon to the Communists. South Vietnam surrenders unconditionally.

1976:
Mar: Harold Wilson announces his resignation as Prime Minister and James Callaghan is elected to the position in April.

Oct: The Intercity 125 high speed passenger train is introduced. Initially Paddington to Bristol and south Wales.

1977:
Jan: Jimmy Carter is sworn in as the 39th President of the United States, succeeding Gerald Ford.

Sep: Freddie Laker launches his 'Skytrain' with a single fare, Gatwick to New York, at £59 compared to £189.

1978:
Aug: Louise Brown becomes the world's first human born 'in vitro fertilisation' – test tube baby.

Nov: An industrial dispute shuts down The Times newspaper – until November 1979.

1979:
Mar: Airey Neave, politician and WW2 veteran, is blown up in the House of Commons carpark by the Irish National Liberation Army.

May: Margaret Thatcher becomes the first female Prime Minister of the United Kingdom. The Conservatives win a 43 seat majority.

THE HOME

Increasing Comfort and Prosperity

Homes became brighter and more comfortable in the 1970's. Teenagers could lie on the 'impossible to clean', loopy shag pile carpet watching films on VHS video cassettes or watch live programmes on the family's colour television set.

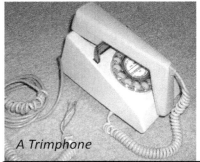

A Trimphone

The ubiquitous macramé owl, or plant holder complete with trailing spider plant, might dangle in the corner adjacent to the bulky, stone faced, rustic fireplace. Bathroom suites were often Avocado green and 'downstairs loos' were a statement of the houseowners ideals! If you were one of the 35% of households in Britain to own a telephone, you could catch up with friends and family on the new 'warbling' Trimphone, maybe sitting on your bright, floral covered couch.

Labour Saving Devices

The previous decade had been prosperous and the advances in technology continued such that by the 1970s, most households had many labour-saving devices. Sales of freezers rose rapidly in the 70s and by 1974, one in ten households had a freezer - mainly full of peas, chips and fish fingers but also ice cream, previously a rare treat, and in large quantities. Bulk buying food meant less time shopping and the Magimix food processor which added a choice of blades and attachments to a standard liquidiser, made home cooking more adventurous.

Teenage Home Entertainment

Teenagers covered their bedroom walls with posters of their favourite bands and actors, ranging from Rod Stewart and the Boomtown Rats to Olivia Newton-John and Robert Redford. The lucky ones listening to top ten singles on their own stereo record deck which had replaced the old Dansette player.

If they wanted to play the new video games, they typically went to an arcade, but in 1975, Atari PONG was released, the first commercially successful video game you could play at home on your television. Based on a simple two-dimensional graphical representation of a tennis-like game, two players used paddles to hit a ball back and forth on a black and white screen. It captivated audiences and its success influenced developers to invent more and increasingly sophisticated games for the home market.

The luxury of a Goblin Teasmade, the automatic tea-maker and alarm clock, revolutionised early morning tea.

1970 - 1974

1970 Laurence Olivier becomes the first actor to be made a Lord. He is given a life peerage in the Queen's Birthday Honours list.

The first Glastonbury Festival was held, called the Worthy Farm Pop Festival. About 1500 attended.

1971 Coco Chanel, the French fashion designer died. (Born 1883)

The 'Blue Peter' presenters buried a time capsule in the grounds of BBC Television Centre, due to be opened on the first episode in 2000.

Mr Tickle, the first of the Mr Men books is published.

1972 'Jesus Christ Superstar', the Tim Rice & Andrew Lloyd Webber musical opens in the West End.

John Betjeman is appointed Poet Laureate.

1973 The British Library is established by merger of the British Museum Library & the National Lending Library for Science & Technology.

Series 1 of the BBC sitcom, 'Last of the Summer Wine' begins. There are eventually, 31 series.

1974 'Tinker, Tailor, Soldier, Spy' the first of John Le Carré's novel featuring the ageing spymaster, George Smiley, is published.

The Terracotta Army of Qin Shi Huang, thousands of life-size clay models of soldiers, horses and chariots, is discovered at Xi'an in China.

Milton Keynes Shopping Centre

1975 - 1979

1975 Donald Coggan is enthroned as the Archbishop of Canterbury.

Bill Gates and Paul Allen found Microsoft in Albuquerque, New Mexico.

1976 Trevor Nunn's memorable production of 'Macbeth' opens at Stratford-upon-Avon, with Ian McKellan and Judi Dench in the lead roles.

The Royal National Theatre on the South Bank opens.

Agatha Christie's last novel, Sleeping Murder, a Miss Marple story is published posthumously.

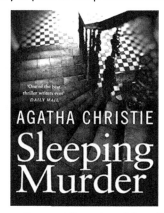

1977 Luciano Pavarotti makes his television debut singing in Puccini's La Boheme in the television debut of 'Live from the Met'.

Mike Leigh's satire on the aspirations and tastes of the new middle class emerging in the 70's, 'Abigail's Party', opened at the Hampstead Theatre starring Alison Steadman.

1978 The Andrew Lloyd Webber musical 'Evita' opens in London.

The arcade video game, 'Space Invaders' is released.

1979 Margaret Thatcher opens the new Central Milton Keynes Shopping Centre, the largest indoor shopping centre in Britain.

Anthony Blunt, British art historian and former Surveyor of the Queen's Pictures, in exposed as a double agent for the Soviets during WW2.

The Sony Walkman, portable cassette player is released.

Pavarotti at the Met.

It was in his third season at the Metropolitan Opera House in New York that Luciano Pavarotti, the operatic tenor, would skyrocket to stardom. The company imported Covent Garden's production of Donizetti's *La Fille du Régiment* in 1972 as a vehicle for Joan Sutherland. The great Australian diva enjoyed a huge triumph, but the surprise for the audience was the young Italian tenor by her side who shared an equal part in the phenomenal success. This was the historic first Met performance telecast live on PBS as part of the long-running series that continues to the present day.

The Terracotta Army

'The Qin Tomb Terracotta Warriors and Horses' was constructed between 246-206BC as an afterlife guard for China's First Emperor, Qin Shihuang, from whom, China gets its name. He ordered it built to remember the army he led to triumph over other warring states, and to unite China.

The tomb and the army were all made by hand by some 700,000 artisans and labourers, and comprises thousands of life-size soldiers, each with different facial features and expressions, clothing, hairstyles and gestures, arranged in battle array.

All figures face east, towards the ancient enemies of Qin State, in rectangular formations and three separate vaults include rows of kneeling and standing archers, chariot war configurations and mixed forces of infantry, horse drawn chariots plus numerous soldiers armed with long spears, daggers and halberds.

FILMS

1970 - 1974

1970 Love Story, was the biggest grossing film a sentimental, tearjerker with the oft-quoted tagline, "Love means never having to say you're sorry." Nominated for the Academy Awards Best Picture, it was beaten by **Patton** which won 7 major titles that year.

1971 The Oscar winner was **The French Connection** with Gene Hackman as a New York police detective, Jimmy 'Popeye' Doyle, chasing down drug smugglers. Hackman was at the peak of his career in the 70's.

1972 Francis Ford Coppola's gangster saga, **The Godfather** became the highest grossing film of its time and helped drive a resurgence in the American film industry.

1973 Glenda Jackson won Best Actress for her role in **A Touch of Class.** She revealed that she was approached for the part by the director after appearing in the 1971 'Antony & Cleopatra' sketch on the Morecambe & Wise show. After she won, Eric Morecambe sent her a telegram saying, "Stick with us and we will get you another one".

1974 New films this year included **The Godfather Part II,** which won the Oscar, **Blazing Saddles** the comedy western and the disaster film, **The Towering Inferno** starring Paul Newman and Steve McQueen.

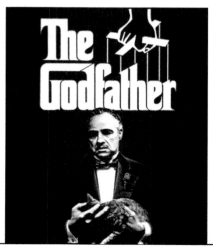

1975 - 1979

1975 One Flew Over the Cuckoo's Nest, an allegorical film set in a mental hospital, starring Jack Nicholson, beat tough competition for Best Picture from Spielberg's **Jaws** and Altman's **Nashville.**

1976 Jodi Foster won an Oscar in Martin Scorsese's gritty film **Taxi Driver** which examines alienation in urban society but it was Sylvester Stallone's **Rocky** that carried off the Best Picture award.

1977 Annie Hall from Woody Allen, the winner of Best Picture is a masterpiece of witty and quotable one-liners.

1978 The Vietnam War is examined through the lives of three friends from a small steel-mill town before, during and after their service in **The Deer Hunter**. A powerful and disturbing film.

1979 In this year's Best Picture, **Kramer v Kramer** there is a restaurant scene where Dustin Hoffman throws his wine glass at the wall. Only the cameraman was forewarned, Meryl Streep's shocked reaction was genuine!

In The 1970s

Star Wars

Star Wars all began with George Lucas's eponymous film in 1977. The epic space fantasy, telling the adventures of characters "A long time ago in a galaxy far, far away", and this first film was a world beater in special effects technology using new computerised and digital effects. It rapidly became a phenomenon, Luke Skywalker, Jedi Knights, Princess Leia and Darth Vader becoming household names. An immensely valuable franchise grew up to include the films, television series, video games, books, comics and theme parks which now amounts to billions of dollars and the film introduced the phrase "May the Force be with you" into common usage.

Apocalypse Now

Joseph Conrad's book 'Heart of Darkness' was the inspiration for producer and director Francis Ford Coppola's psychological film, a metaphor for the madness and folly of war itself for a generation of young American men. Beautiful, with symbolic shots showing the confusion, violence and fear of the nightmare of the Vietnam War, much of it was filmed on location in the Philippines where expensive sets were destroyed by severe weather, a typhoon called 'Olga', Marlon Brando showed up on set overweight and completely unprepared and Martin Sheen had a near-fatal heart attack.

This led to the film being two and a half times over budget and taking twice the number of scheduled weeks to shoot. When filming finally finished, the release was postponed several times as Coppola had six hours of film to edit. The helicopter attack scene with the 'Ride of the Valkyries' soundtrack is one of the most memorable film scenes ever.

Women Wear the Trousers

It is often said that 1970s styles had no direction and were too prolific. French couture no longer handed down diktats of what we should be wearing, and the emerging street style was inventive, comfortable, practical for women or glamorous. It could be home-made, it was whatever you wanted it to be, and the big new trend was for gender neutral clothes, women wore trousers in every walk of life, trouser suits for the office, jeans at home and colourful, tight-fitting ones for in between. Trouser legs became wider and 'bell-bottoms', flared from the knee down, with bottom leg openings of up to twenty-six inches, made from denim, bright cotton and satin polyester, became mainstream. Increasingly 'low cut', they were teamed with platform soles or high cut boots until they could not flare anymore, and so, by the end of the decade they had gone, skin-tight trousers, in earth tones, greys, whites and blacks were much more in vogue.

And the Hot Pants

In the early 70s, women's styles were very flamboyant with extremely bright colours and, in the winter, long, flowing skirts and trousers *but* come the summer, come the Hot Pants. These extremely short shorts were made of luxury fabrics such as velvet and satin designed for fashionable wear, not the practical equivalents for sports or leisure, and they enjoyed great popularity until falling out of fashion in the middle of the decade. Teamed with skin-tight t-shirts, they were favourites for clubwear and principally worn by women, including Jacqueline Kennedy Onassis, Elizabeth Taylor and Jane Fonda, but they were also worn by some high-profile men, David Bowie, Sammy Davis Jnr and Liberace among them, although the shorts were slightly longer than the women's versions, but still shorter than usual. Chest hair, medallions, sideburns and strangely, tennis headbands, finished the look!

These Boots Are Made For Walking

Boots were so popular in the early 1970s that even men were getting in on the action. It wasn't uncommon to see a man sporting 2" inch platform boots inspired by John Travolta in Saturday Night Fever. The trend was all about being sexy on the dance floor!

And Punk Was Not to Be Ignored

Emerging in the mid 70s in London as an anarchic and aggressive movement, a few hundred young people defined themselves as an anti-fashion urban youth street culture closely aligned to the music that became punk. They cut up old clothes from charity shops, destroyed the fabric and refashioned outfits in a manner intended to shock. Trousers were deliberately torn to reveal laddered tights and dirty legs and worn with heavy Doc Martens footwear, now seen on many young women too.

Safety pins and chains held bits of fabric together. Neck chains were made from padlocks and chain and even razor blades were used as pendants. Body piercings and studs, beginning with the three-stud earlobe, progressing to the ear outline embedded with ear studs, evolved to pins in eyebrows, cheeks, noses or lips and together with tattoos were the beginning of unisex fashion. All employed by male and female alike to offend. Vivienne Westwood and Malcolm McLaren quickened the style with her bondage shop "Sex", and his punk music group, the "Sex Pistols".

Saturday Morning TV

In the early 70s, Saturday mornings for many children still meant a trip to the cinema but with the advent of Saturday Morning Television, under instruction 'not to wake their parents', children could creep downstairs, switch on the box and stay entertained until lunchtime.

First, in 1974, came ITV's 'Tiswas', hosted by Chris Tarrant it was a chaotic blend of jokes, custard pies and buckets of water.

Then in 1976, the BBC introduced 'Swap Shop' with Noel Edmonds, Keith Chegwin and John Craven and a Saturday morning ritual was born. Nearly three hours of ground-breaking television using the 'phone-in' extensively for the first time on TV. The programme included music, competitions, cartoons and spontaneous nonsense from Edmonds. There was coverage of news and issues relevant to children, presented by 'Newsround's' John Craven but by far the most popular element of the show was the "Swaporama" open-air event, hosted by Chegwin. An outside broadcast unit would travel to different locations throughout the UK where sometimes as many as 2000 children would gather to swap their belongings with others.

Saturday Night Fever

Memories of Saturday night and Sunday morning in the discotheque. A mirror ball; strobe lights; 'four on the floor' rhythm; the throb of the bass drum; girls in Spandex tops with hot pants or vividly coloured, shiny, Lycra trousers with equally dazzling halter neck tops; boys in imitations of John Travolta's white suit from Saturday Night Fever risking life and limb on towering platform shoes.

These glamorous dancers, clad in glitter, metallic lame and sequins, gyrating as the music pounded out at the direction of the DJ, whirling energetically and glowing bright 'blue-white' under the ultra-violet lights as their owners 'strutted their stuff', perspiration running in rivulets down their backs.

The DJs, stars in their own right, mixed tracks by Donna Summer, the Bee Gees, Gloria Gaynor, Sister Sledge, Chic and Chaka Khan, as their sexy followers, fuelled by the night club culture of alcohol and drugs, changed from dancing the Hustle with their partners to the solo freestyle dancing of John Travolta.

The Dangers of Leisure

In the 1970's the Government was intent on keeping us all – and particularly children – safe and continued producing the wartime Public Information Films, which were still scaring children witless!

1971: Children and Disused Fridges: Graphic warnings of children being suffocated in old fridges that, tempted by their playful imaginations, they want to climb into.

1973: Broken Glass: This film shows a boy running on the sand, ending abruptly before he steps on a broken glass bottle, the film urges people to use a bin or take their litter home with them.

1974: The Fatal Floor: This 30 second film had the message, "Polish a floor, put a rug on it, and you might as well set a man trap…"

1979: Play Safe – Frisbee: This film used chilling electronic music and frightening sound effects to highlight the potentially fatal combination of frisbees with electricity pylons and kites, fishing rods and radio-controlled planes.

1972: Teenagers – Learn to Swim:

A cartoon aimed at teenagers warns them to learn how to swim, or risk social embarrassment and failure to attract the opposite sex. The female character's illusion of her boyfriend 'Dave' being able 'to do anything' is shattered after she wishes they were at the seaside, where she discovers Dave can't swim. He in turn wishes he didn't 'keep losing me birds' after his girlfriend disappears with 'Mike' who 'swims like a fish'. Although the film is light-hearted in tone it was intended in part to help prevent accidents.

1975: Protect and Survive:

This was the title of a series of booklets and films made in the late 1970s and early 1980s, dealing with emergency planning for a nuclear war including the recognition of attack warning, fallout warning, and all-clear signals, the preparation of a home "fallout room" and the stockpiling of food, water, and other emergency supplies. In the opinion of some contemporary critics, the films *were deeply and surprisingly fatalistic in tone*!

MUSIC

1970 - 1974

1970 Number 1 for 3 weeks, **Bridge Over Troubled Water** by Simon and Garfunkel became their 'signature song' selling over 6m copies worldwide. It also became one of the most performed songs of the 20th century, covered by over 50 artists.

1971 George Harrison's first release as a solo **My Sweet Lord** topped the charts for five weeks and became the best selling UK single of the year.
Rod Stewart had 7 No 1's this year including in October, the double sided hits, **Reason to Believe/Maggie May**

ROD STEWART
MAGGIE MAY The Essential Collection

1972 A jingle, rewritten to become the hugely popular 'Buy the world a Coke' advert for the Coca Cola company, was re-recorded by The New Seekers as the full-length song, **I'd Like to Teach the World to Sing**, which stayed at No 1 for 4 weeks.

1973 Dawn featuring Tony Orlando had the bestselling single of 1973 with **"Tie a Yellow Ribbon Round the 'Ole Oak Tree"**, which spent four weeks at the top spot and lasted 11 weeks in the top ten.
Queen released their debut album, **"Queen"**. The Carpenters reached number 2 with **"Yesterday Once More"**.

1974 Waterloo, the winning song for Sweden in the Eurovision Song Contest began ABBA's journey to world-wide fame.
David Essex has his first No 1 with **Wanna Make You a Star** which spends 3 weeks at the top of the charts.

1975 - 1979

1975 Make Me Smile (Come Up and See Me) was a chart topper for Steve Harley & Cockney Rebel. **Bohemian Rhapsody** for Queen, stayed at the top for nine weeks.

1976 The Brotherhood of Man won the Eurovision Song Contest for Great Britain with **Save Your Kisses for Me**. It became the biggest-selling song of the year and remains one of the biggest-selling Eurovision winners ever.
Don't Go Breaking My Heart was the first No. 1 single in the UK for both Elton John and Kiki Dee.

1977 Actor David Soul, riding high on his success in Starsky & Hutch, had the No 1 spot for 4 weeks with **Don't Give Up on Us**.
Way Down was the last song to be recorded by Elvis Presley before his death and stayed at No 1 for 5 weeks.

KATE BUSH
WUTHERING HEIGHTS

1978 Kate Bush released her debut single, **Wuthering Heights,** which she had written aged 18 after watching Emily Brontë's Wuthering Heights on television and discovering she shared the author's birthday.
Spending five weeks at the top of the British charts, Boney M's **"Rivers of Babylon"** became the biggest selling single of the year, exceeding one million sales between May and June.

1979 Frequently recalled as a symbol of female empowerment, **I Will Survive** reached the top for Gloria Gaynor.
The Wall, Pink Floyd's rock opera was released, featuring all three parts of **Another Brick in the Wall. Part 2**, written as a protest against rigid schooling was No1 in Dec.

The Decade in Numbers

Most No1 Singles:
ABBA with seven.
Waterloo (1974);
Mamma Mia, Fernando and
Dancing Queen (all 1976);
Knowing Me Knowing You, The Name of the Game, (both 1977);
Take a Chance on Me (1978).

Most Weeks at No 1:
Bohemian Rhapsody by Queen; **Mull of Kintyre / Girl's School** by Wings; **You're the One That I Want** by John Travolta and Olivia Newton-John.

WINGS

MULL OF KINTYRE

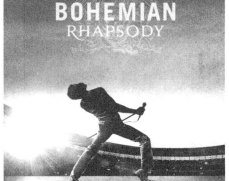

'Danny' and 'Sandy' Fever

Grease, the 1978 musical romantic comedy starring John Travolta (Danny) and Olivia Newton-John (Sandy) had phenomenal success. In June to August 1978, **You're the One That I Want** and in September to October, **Summer Nights**, locked up the number 1 position for a total of sixteen weeks.

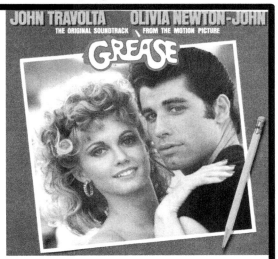

Hopelessly Devoted to You was nominated for an Oscar and John Travolta and Olivia Newton-John seemed to be constantly in the public conscience. Critically and commercially successful, the soundtrack album ended 1978 as the second best-selling album in the US, behind the soundtrack of the 1977 blockbuster **Saturday Night Fever,** which also starred John Travolta.

Pocket Calculators

The first pocket calculators came onto the market towards the end of 1970. In the early 70s they were an expensive status symbol but by the middle of the decade, businessmen were quite used to working their sales figures out quickly whilst 'out of the office'.

Household accounts were made easy and children wished they could use them at school – not just to help with homework. Most early calculators performed only basic addition, subtraction, multiplication and division but the speed and accuracy, sometimes giving up to 12 digit answers, of the machine proved sensational.

In 1972, Hewlett Packard introduced the revolutionary HP-35 pocket calculator which, in addition to the basic operations, enabled advanced mathematical functions. It was the first scientific, hand-held calculator, able to perform a wide number of logarithmic and trigonometric functions, store intermediate solutions and utilise scientific notations.

With intense competition, prices of pocket calculators dropped rapidly, and the race was on to produce the smallest possible models. The target was to be no bigger than a credit card. Casio won the race.

The Miracle of IVF

In 1971, Patrick Steptoe, gynaecologist, Robert Edwards, biologist, and Jean Purdy, nurse and embryologist set up a small laboratory at the Kershaw's Hospice in Oldham which was to lead to the development of in vitro fertilisation and eventual birth of Louise Brown in 1978.

They developed a technique for retrieving eggs at the right time and fertilising them in the laboratory, believing that they could be implanted back in the uterus. It took more than 80 embryo transfers before the first successful pregnancy, and the birth of Louise, the first 'test-tube baby', heralded the potential happiness of infertile people and a bright future for British science andindustry.

In The 1970s

"Houston We Have a Problem"

In April 1970, two days after the launch of Apollo 13, the seventh crewed mission in the Apollo space program and the third meant to land on the Moon, the NASA ground crew heard the now famous message, "Houston, we've had a problem." An oxygen tank had exploded, and the lunar landing was aborted leaving the astronauts in serious danger. The crew looped around the Moon and returned safely to Earth, their safe return being down to the ingenuity under pressure by the crew, commanded by Jim Lovell, together with the flight controllers and mission control. The crew experienced great hardship, caused by limited power, a chilly and wet cabin and a shortage of drinking water.

Even so, Apollo 13 set a spaceflight record for the furthest humans have travelled from Earth.

Tens of millions of viewers watched Apollo 13 splashdown in the South Pacific Ocean and the recovery by USS Iwo Jima.

The global campaigning network **Greenpeace** was founded in 1971 by Irving and Dorothy Stowe, environmental activists. The network now has 26 independent national or regional organisations in 55 countries worldwide.

Their stated goal is to ensure the ability of the earth to nurture life in all its diversity. To achieve this they "use non-violent, creative confrontation to expose global environmental problems, and develop solutions for a green and peaceful future". In detail to:

- Stop the planet from warming beyond 1.5° in order to prevent the most catastrophic impacts of the climate breakdown.
- Protect biodiversity in all its forms.
- Slow the volume of hyper-consumption and learn to live within our means.
- Promote renewable energy as a solution that can power the world.
- Nurture peace, global disarmament and non-violence.

SPORT

1970 - 1974

1970 The thoroughbred 'Nijinsky', wins all three English Triple Crown Races: **The 2,000 Guineas** at Newmarket; **The Derby** at Epsom; the **St. Leger Stakes** at Doncaster and the Irish Derby. The first horse to do this in 35 years and not repeated as of 2021.

1971 Arsenal wins both the **First Division** title and the **FA Cup**, becoming the fourth team ever to win the double.
Jack Nicklaus wins his ninth major at the **PGA Championship**, the first golfer ever to win all four majors for the second time.

1972 At **Wimbledon**, Stan Smith (US) beat Ilie Nastase in the Men's Singles Final. It was his only Wimbledon title.
In the Women's Final, Billie Jean King (US) beat Yvonne Goolagong (AUS) to gain her fourth **Wimbledon** title.
The **Olympic Games** held in Munich are overshadowed by the murder of eleven Israeli athletes and coaches by Palestinian Black September members.

1973 George Foreman knocks out Joe Frazier in only two rounds to take the **World Heavyweight Boxing** Championship title.

Red Rum wins the **Grand National** with a new record and staging a spectacular comeback on the run-in having trailed the leader by 15 lengths at the final fence.

1974 Liverpool win the **FA Cup Final** against Newcastle United at Wembley. Kevin Keegan scored two of their three goals.
Eddie Merckx wins the **Tour de France**, becoming the first rider to win the Triple Crown of Cycling, **Tour de France**, **Giro d'Italia** and **World Championships** in one calendar year.

1975 - 1979

1975 In athletics, John Walker (NZ) sets a new world record becoming the first man to **run a mile** in under 3 mins 50 seconds. He clocks 3mins 49.4 secs.
Muhammad Ali defeats Joe Frazier in the 'Thrilla In Manilla' to maintain the **Boxing Heavyweight Championship** of the world.

1976 The **Olympics** are held in Montreal. Britain's only medal is a Bronze, won by Brendan Foster running the **10,000 metres**.
John Curry, becomes the **European, Olympic and World Figure Skating Champion**. He was the first skater to combine, ballet and modern dance into his skating.

1977 The commercial **World Series Cricket** was introduced by Kerry Packer. WSC changed the nature of the game with its emphasis on the "gladiatorial" aspect of fast bowling and heavy promotion of fast bowlers.

1978 During the **Oxford and Cambridge Boat Race,** the Cambridge boat sinks. It is the first sinking in the race since 1951.
Wales wins the rugby **Five Nations Championship** and completes the Grand Slam having beaten England, France, Ireland and Scotland.

1978 Arsenal beat Manchester United 3-2 in the **FA Cup Final.**
At **The Open** at Royal Lytham & St Annes Golf Club Seve Ballesteros becomes the first golfer from Continental Europe to win a major since 1907.

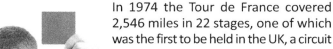

Traffic Lights and Football

Before the introduction of Red and Yellow Cards in football, cautions or sending a player off had to be dealt with orally, and the language barrier could sometimes present problems. For example, in the 1966 World Cup, the German referee tried in vain to send Argentinian player Antonio Rattin off the field, but Rattin did not 'want' to understand and eventually was escorted off the pitch by the police! Ken Aston, Head of World Cup Referees, was tasked with solving this problem and legend has it that the idea of the red and yellow cards came to him when he was stopped in his car at traffic lights. They were tested in the 1968 Olympics and the 1970 World Cup in Mexico and introduced to European leagues soon after and after six years, to English football.

In 1976, the first player to be sent off using a red card in an English game was Blackburn Rovers winger David Wagstaffe.

Tour de France

In 1974 the Tour de France covered 2,546 miles in 22 stages, one of which was the first to be held in the UK, a circuit stage on the Plympton By-pass near Plymouth. Eddy Merckx of Belgium won eight stages and won the race overall with a comfortable margin, making it five wins for him out of his five Tours. He also won that year's Combination Classification – the General (Yellow Jersey), Points or Sprint (Green Jersey) and Mountains (since 1975, King of the Mountains wears the Polka Dot Jersey).

Rockstar and Racing Driver

James Hunt, the charismatic, play-boy darling of the press in the 1970's, began his Formula 1 career at the beginning of the decade with the Hesketh Racing team and gave them their only win in 1975 at the Dutch GP. He moved to McLaren in 1976, and in his first year with them, he and his great rival Niki Lauda at Ferrari, fought an epic season-long battle. It was an extraordinarily dramatic season, over sixteen races filled with drama and controversy, where Lauda had gained an early championship lead. By the final race in Japan, he was being reeled-in by Hunt and was only three points ahead. Hunt drove the race of his life, in the worst possible weather conditions, to finish in third place. Lauda, already badly injured from the crash at Nürburgring in August, withdrew because of the hazardous conditions which meant James Hunt became World Champion, winning by just a single point.

Hunt's natural driving ability was phenomenal, and while his habit of risk-taking didn't always endear him to others, hence the nickname "Hunt the Shunt", it also made him compelling to watch. Off track, he and Niki had an enduring friendship, which lasted after James's retirement from F1 in 1979 until his untimely death from a heart attack in 1993, aged just 45.

ICONIC MACHINES OF THE DECADE

The Jumbo Jet
Entered service on January 22, 1970. The 747 was the first airplane dubbed a "Jumbo Jet", the first wide-body airliner.

In 1971 Ford launched the car that was to represent the 1970s, the Cortina Mk III. In 1976 the Mk IV and 1979 Mk V. Cortinas were the best-selling cars of the decade.

The best-selling foreign import was the Datsun Sunny, which was only the 19th best-selling car of the decade.

In 1973, British Leyland's round, dumpy shaped Allegro was not at all popular and meagre sales contributed greatly to BL's collapse in 1975.

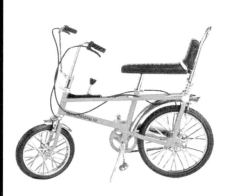

Raleigh Chopper
Shot to fame in the 70's when every child, and some adults, wanted one. It had a high back, long seat and motorbike rear wheel and was probably the first bike to have a centrally positioned gear shift.

Women Drivers

In 1974, Jill Viner became the first female bus driver for London Transport. She trained to become a bus driver at a centre in Chiswick in 1974, when London Transport were said to be 3,200 drivers short

While women had previously driven buses within bus depots during the Second World War, Viner was the first women to drive a bus in service in London. In the weeks after she started driving, it was reported that thirty women had applied to become bus drivers.

In 1978, Hannah Dadds completed a seven-week training course to qualify as a train driver and became the first female driver on the London Underground.

Hannah's sister Edna also joined the London Underground working first as a guard and then a driver. Hannah and Edna became the first all-female crew on the London Underground.

Concorde

The Anglo-French supersonic passenger airliner had a take-off speed of 220 knots (250mph) and a cruising speed of 1350mph – more than twice the speed of sound. With seating for 92 to 128 passengers, Concorde entered service in 1976 and operated for 27 years.

Twenty aircraft were built in total, including six prototypes and in the end, only Air France and British Airways purchased and flew them, due in great part to supersonic flights being restricted to ocean-crossing routes, to prevent sonic boom disturbance over land and populated areas. Concorde flew regular transatlantic flights from London and Paris to New York, Washington, Dulles in Virginia and Barbados and the BA Concorde made just under 50,000 flights and flew more than 2.5m passengers supersonically.

A typical London to New York crossing would take a little less than three and a half hours as opposed to about eight hours for a subsonic flight.

The aircraft was retired in 2003, three years after the crash of an Air France flight in which all passengers and crew were killed.

THE MAJOR NEWS STORIES

1980 - 1984

1980:

May: Mount St. Helens experiences a huge eruption that creates avalanches, explosions, large ash clouds, mudslides, and massive damage. 57 people are killed.

Dec: John Lennon, the former Beatle, age 40, is shot and killed by an obsessed fan in Manhattan.

1981:

July: Prince Charles marries Lady Diana Spencer at St Paul's Cathedral.

Margaret Thatcher's Government begins the privatisation of the Nationalised Industries.

1982:

Apr: Argentina invades the Falkland Islands and the UK retakes possession of them by the end of June.

May: Pope John Paul II visits the United Kingdom. It is the first visit by a reigning Pope

1983:

Apr: The £1 coin is introduced in the UK.

Jun: Margaret Thatcher wins a landslide victory for the Conservatives in the General Election, with a majority of 144.

Nov: The first United States cruise missiles arrive at RAF Greenham Common in Berkshire

1984:

Mar: The National Mineworkers Union led by Arthur Scargill, begin what will be a year-long strike against the National Coal Board's plans to shut 20 collieries

May: The Thames Barrier, designed to protect London from floods, is opened by9The Queen

1980: Mount St. Helens before and after the eruption. The top third of the mountain was blown away.

1982: EPCOT opened at Disney World in Florida, "...an experimental prototype community of tomorrow that will take its cue from the new ideas and technologies that are now emerging ... a showcase of the ingenuity and imagination of American free enterprise." - *Walt Disney*

1984: On 31 October, Indira Gandhi, Prime Minister of India, was killed by her Sikh bodyguards.
The assassination sparked four days of riots that left more than 8,000 Indian Sikhs dead in revenge attacks.

1985 - 1989

1985: On 1st January, Ernie Wise made the first, civilian, mobile phone call in the UK from outside the Dicken's Inn at St Katharine's Dock. Via the Vodafone network he called their office in Newbury on a VT1 which weighed 5.5kg.

1985:

Jan: The Internet's Domain Name System is created and the country code top-level domain .uk is registered in July.

Dec: The original charity "Comic Relief" is launched by Richard Curtis and Lenny Henry on Christmas Day,.

1986:

Apr: A Soviet Nuclear reactor at Chernobyl explodes causing the release of radioactive material across much of Europe.

Oct: The 'Big Bang' – the London Stock Exchange is deregulated allowing computerised share dealing.

1987:

Jan: Terry Waite, the special envoy of the Archbishop of Canterbury in Lebanon, is kidnapped in Beirut. He is held in captivity for 1,763 days until 1991.

Oct: Black Monday: Wall Street crash leads to £50,000,000,000 being wiped of the value of shares on the London stock exchange.

1988:

Dec: Suspected Libyan terrorist bomb explodes on Pan Am jet over Lockerbie in Scotland on December 21st killing all 259 on board and 11 on the ground.

Dec: Health Minister Edwina Currie states that most of Britain's egg production is infected with salmonella, causing an immediate nationwide slump in egg sales.

1989:

Apr: 94 fans are killed in the Hillsborough football stadium collapse in Sheffield. 3 more will die and over 300 are hospitalised.

Nov: The Fall of the Berlin Wall heralds the end of the Cold War and communism in East and Central Europe.

1987: Oct 15th: Weather-man Michael Fish: "Earlier on today, a woman rang the BBC and said she heard there was a hurricane on the way... well, if you're watching, don't worry, there isn't!". That night, hurricane force winds hit much of the South of England killing 23 people, bringing down an estimated 15 million trees and causing damage estimated at £7.3 billion.

THE HOME

A Busier Life

In the 1980's, life became more stressful, there were two recessions, divorce rates were increasing, women were exercising their rights and these years were the beginning of the end of the traditional family unit. With single parent families or both parents at work and a generally 'busier' life, there was a fundamental change to the family and home. There was also a lot more choice.

Many more 'lower cost' restaurants, chilled ready-made meals, instant foods such as Findus Crispy Pancakes, Pot Noodles or M&S Chicken Kievs and the, by now, ubiquitous tea bag, together with the consumer boom in electrical labour-saving devices from food processors and microwaves to dishwashers and automatic washing machines, sandwich toasters and jug kettles, all added up to more free time from housework and cooking.

Floral Décor

Flower patterns were all the rage in early 1980s home décor, with flower patterned upholstery and curtains to floral wallpapers taking over from the 70s woodchip paper.

Artex was still hugely popular on ceilings and walls, finished with the familiar stippled or swirled patterns and peach was *the* fashionable colour of choice for interior design schemes. Chintz curtains could have more layers, swags and tails than an onion! The bold reached the height of fashion with a red and black colour scheme, black ash furniture and a framed Ferrari print on the wall – with a bold wallpaper border at the ceiling which often clashed with the paper on the walls.

The Telephone Answering Machine

There once was a time when, to use a telephone, both people had to be on the phone at the same time. You had to pick up the phone when it rang. The answering machine, one cassette tape for the outgoing message and one to record incoming calls, changed all that. By allowing people to take calls when they were away and respond to any message at a later time.

Children's Playtime

For children, toys of the early 80s had a bit of a 70s feel, Star Wars action figures, remote controlled cars and trucks, Barbie dolls and Action Men, but by 1983 there was a huge increase in toys like Transformers, Care Bears, a plethora of talking robot toys, My Little Pony, Teenage Mutant Ninja Turtles and Cabbage Patch Kids which was THE craze of 1983 – these odd looking 'little people' were the first images to feature on disposable 'designer' nappies!

Basic Atari video games evolved to Nintendo's NES game system and all of them competed with Apple and Sinclair home computers and personal Walkman stereos.

ART AND CULTURE

1980 - 1984

1980 "Who shot J.R.?" was an advertising catchphrase that CBS created to promote their TV show, 'Dallas', referring to the cliff hanger of the finale of the previous season. The episode, 'Who Done It?' aired in November with an estimated 83 million viewers tuning in.

MV Mi Amigo, the ship 'Radio Caroline', the pirate radio station, operates from, runs aground and sinks off Sheerness.

1981 A bronze statue of Charlie Chaplin, as his best loved character, The Tramp, is unveiled in Leicester Square.

1982 The D'Oyly Carte Opera Company gives its last performance at the end of a final London season, having been in near-continuous existence since 1875.

1983 Children's ITV is launched in Britain as a new branding for the late afternoon programming block on the ITV network.

1984 The comedian Tommy Cooper collapses and dies on stage from a heart attack during a live televised show, 'Live from Her Majesty's'.

Ted Hughes is appointed Poet Laureate and succeeds Sir John Betjeman. Philip Larkin had turned down the post.

1985 - 1989

1985 The Roux Brothers' Waterside Inn at Bray, Berkshire becomes the first establishment in the UK to be awarded three Michelin stars.

'Live Aid' pop concerts in London and Philadelphia raise over £50,000,000 for famine relief in Ethiopia.

1986 The Sun newspaper alleges that comedian Freddie Starr ate a live hamster.

More than 30m viewers watched the Christmas Day episode of 'East Enders' in which Den Watts serves the divorce papers on his wife Angie.

1987 Christie's auction house in London sells one of Vincent van Gogh's iconic Sunflowers paintings for £24,750,000 after a bidding war between two unidentified competitors bidding via telephone.

'The Simpsons' cartoon first appears as a series of animated short films on the 'Tracey Ullman Show' in the US.

1988 Salman Rushdie published 'The Satanic Verses' a work of fiction which caused a widespread furore and forced Rushdie to live in hiding out of fear for his life.

1989 Sky Television begins broadcasting as the first satellite TV service in Britain.

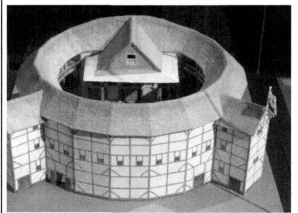

Remains of both The Rose, an Elizabethan playhouse, and the Globe Theatre are found in London.

The Great Musical Revival

By the start of the 1980's, Britain was in recession and the West End Theatres were facing rising costs and falling audiences – until the revival of the Musical, led by Andrew Lloyd Webber.

In 1981, his first 'unlikely' musical **Cats** led by Elaine Paige, went on to be the first 'megamusical' spectacular in the West End and on Broadway.

It was followed in 1984 by **Starlight Express.**

By now, these shows were being enjoyed not only by home audiences but also, a massive 44% of tickets, were purchased by tourists.

In 1986, the **Phantom of the Opera** opened to overwhelmingly positive reviews.

In 1987 **Les Misérables** brought the Royal Shakespeare Company 's expertise in high drama to the musical which was set amidst the French Revolution and brought fame to its writers, Alain Boubill and Claude-Michel Schönberg fame and producer Cameron Mackintosh his millions.

Other hit musicals of the decade: Willy Russel's **Blood Brothers**, Noël Gay's revival of **Me and My Girl**, and Lloyd Webber's **Aspects of Love.**

FILMS

1980 - 1984

1980 The epic **The Empire Strikes Back** is released and is the highest-grossing film of the year, just as its predecessor, **Star Wars** was in 1977. However, the Oscar for Best Picture went to **Ordinary People**, the psychological drama depicting the disintegration of an upper middle-class family in Illinois.

1981 Chariots of Fire based on the true story of two British athletes, one Christian, one Jewish in the 1924 Olympics, won the Academy Awards.
The film's title was inspired by the line "Bring me my Chariot of fire!" from Blake's poem adapted as the hymn 'Jerusalem'.

1982 Spielberg's science fiction film of **ET the Extra Terrestrial** was a huge box office hit this year, the scene when the little green extra-terrestrial learns to speak, instilled "ET phone home" into the collective memory. The rather more down to earth biographical film of Mahatma Gandhi **Gandhi**, picked up the Best Film award.

1983 There were many great British films this year including **Local Hero** and **Educating Rita, The Dresser** and Sean Connery playing Bond for the last time in **Never Say Never Again.** It was the American, **Terms of Endearment** that won the Oscars.

1984 Amadeus the fictionalised story of the composer Wolfgang Amadeus Mozart and a supposed rivalry with Italian composer Antonio Salieri, featuring much of Mozart's music, won the imagination of the audiences and the Best Film of the Year award too.

1985 - 1989

1985 Spielberg's 'coming of age' epic starring Whoopi Goldberg in her breakthrough role, **The Color Purple**, was nominated for eleven Academy Awards but failed to achieve a single win. The prize went to Meryl Streep and Robert Redford in the romantic drama, **Out of Africa.**

1986 The first of Oliver Stone's trilogy based on his experiences in the Vietnam war, **Platoon** picks up this year's Oscar for Best Film, beating two British nominations, **A Room with a View** and **The Mission.** This was also the year of the Australian box office runaway success, **Crocodile Dundee.**

1987 The thriller **Fatal Attraction** attracted both favourable reviews and controversy. It put the phrase 'bunny boiler' into the urban dictionary.

1988 Glenn Close was nominated for Best Actress for her role as the Marquise de Merteuil who plots revenge against her ex-lover, in **Dangerous Liaisons.** Dustin Hoffman and Tom Cruise starred in **Rainman**, the winner of Best Film of the year.

1989 Unusually, it was a PG rated film, **Driving Miss Daisy** that won the Academy Award this year, a gentle, heartwarming comedy which had the serious themes of racism and anti-semitism at its heart. Jessica Tandy at age 81, won Best Actress, the oldest winner to do so.

David Puttnam, Baron Puttnam of Queensgate (1997)

The 1980s saw the release of several films by the British producer, David Puttnam, beginning with, in 1981, his most successful film up until that time, **Chariots of Fire**.

His next big success was **Local Hero** the comedy drama, set on the west coast of Scotland where an American oil company wishes to purchase a local village and surrounding area.

Next, in 1984, came the acclaimed **Cal**, a young man on the fringes of the IRA who falls in love with a Catholic woman whose husband, a Protestant policeman, had been killed by the IRA one year earlier. Entered into the Cannes Film Festival, Helen Mirren won Best Actress.

Also in 1984, Puttnam produced **The Killing Fields**, a harrowing biographical drama about the Khmer Rouge in Cambodia, based on the experiences of a Cambodian journalist and an American journalist. This film received seven Oscar nominations and won three, most notably Best Supporting Actor for Haing S. Ngor who had no previous acting experience.

Puttnam's career spanned the 1960s to the 1990s and his films have won 10 Oscars, 31 BAFTAs, 13 Golden Globes, nine Emmys, four David di Donatellos in Italy and the Palme d'Or at Cannes.

FASHION

A Fashion Statement

The mid to late 80s was the time to 'make a statement'. The mass media took over fashion trends completely and fashion magazines, TV shows and music videos all played a part in dictating the latest bold fashions.

There was a huge emphasis on bright colours, huge shoulder pads, power suits which gave an exaggerated silhouette like an upside-down triangle, flashy skirts and spandex leggings, velour, leg warmers and voluminous parachute pants.

We wore iconic oversized plastic hoop earrings, rubber bracelets and shiny chain necklaces and huge sunglasses giving faces the appearance of large flies. Men and women alike made their hair 'big' with or without the ubiquitous teased perm and for the girls, glossy pink lips, overly filled-in brows, rainbow-coloured eyeshadows and exaggerated blusher were on trend.

Men too joined in with style and sported oversized blazers with shiny buttons, pinstripe two-piece suits and sweaters, preferably from Ralph Lauren, draped over the shoulders.

Polka Dots

Although not new to the 80s - Disney's Minnie Mouse was first seen in the 1920's wearing the red and white dottie print - polka dots were also very popular.

Bands such as The Beat used them in their music videos and well-known celebrities including Madonna and Princess Diana loved the cool look of polka dot dresses and tops.

When teamed with the oversized earrings of the decade and big hair, whilst bucking the trend for bright, gaudy colours, they still "made a statement".

Carolina Herrera used polka dots on most of her dresses during the late 1980s and early 1990s and it remains a key print in her collections, a classic.

As Marc Jacobs, the American designer famously said, "There is never a wrong time for a polka dot."

Labels, logos and idols

Pale blue, distressed jeans were the fashionable 'street wear', worn semi fitted and held with a statement belt at the natural waistline. When the boy band Bros came along in 1988, wearing jeans ripped at the knee coupled with leather, slip on loafers, teens up and down the country enthusiastically took the scissors to their own jeans, and ripped, frayed or shredded them.

Pop Fashion
If you were into pop music in the 1980s, there's no doubt that superstar Madonna influenced what you wore.

Feet also presented a branding opportunity, Patrick Cox had celebrities make his loafers universally desired, and, often credited with kicking off the whole fashion sneaker movement, Nike Air 'Jordans' – named after basketball star, Michael Jordan – were launched in 1985. If you couldn't have them, then high-top Reebok sneakers were also the pinnacle of style -- as were Adidas Superstar kicks and matching tracksuits.

The Fitness Craze

The 1980's had a fitness craze. Celebrities made aerobics videos and endorsed weight loss products and equipment. Health Clubs and Gyms became the place to be and to be seen but were predominantly for men so for women who wanted to exercise in the privacy of their own home, by the mid '80s, there were very few households that didn't own at least one well-worn VHS copy of **'Jane Fonda's Workout'**.

Her 1982 video sold more than 17 million copies, with the actress wearing a striped and belted leotard, violet leggings and leg warmers, big, big hair and in full make-up and working up a sweat to some heavy synth music, inspired a whole generation.

At home, between 1983 and 1987, Britain's answer to Jane Fonda, Diana Moran **'The Green Goddess',** appeared on TV screens wearing her trade-mark green leotard telling millions of BBC Breakfast viewers to 'wake up and shape up' with her aerobics routines.

What's On Telly?

Television was a very large part of leisure in the 1980s and with the massive growth in video recorders, the whole family had more control over what they watched and when they watched it.

It was the decade when the huge American 'soaps' **Dallas** and **Dynasty** dominated the ratings and influenced popular debate as well as fashions. In Britain there was a rash of police dramas and the introduction of female detectives in both BBC **'Juliet Bravo'** and ITV **'The Gentle Touch'**. They also covered the land, **'Taggart'** in Scotland, **'Bergerac'** in Jersey, **'The Chinese Detective'** in London and **'Inspector Morse'** in Oxford.

Channel 4 launched in 1982 with its first programme being **'Countdown',** Breakfast TV began in 1983, in 1980s television produced 'historic' shared experiences, **'Who Shot JR'** in Dallas watched by 80 million, the finale of **MASH**, 'Goodbye, Farewell and Amen', by more than 100 million, 30 million tuned in to watch 'Dirty Den' serve his wife 'Angie' with the divorce papers in East Enders and 27 million watched the episode after Alan Bradley tried to kill Rita Fairclough in **Coronation Street**.

What Was New?

Whilst the 80s made huge advances in technology for leisure, Game Boy and Nintendo, VCRs and CDs, disposable cameras and brick shaped mobile phones too, there were other innovations.

In the 'yuppie' years of 'spend, spend, spend', the first smart chip-enabled credit cards were busy being swiped for BMX bikes, Trivial Pursuit and Rubik's Cubes.

Nike told us to 'Just Do It' and we wondered how we'd ever managed without Post-It Notes and disposable contact lenses.

What the world did not want however, was New Coke. Coca Cola changed their classic formula for a sweeter one which received an extremely poor response.

It was one of the worst marketing blunders ever because for the public, this tampered recipe 'Just wasn't it!'. The company brought back the original Coke and sold this new formula as the 'New Coke' till the early 90s.

MUSIC

1980 - 1984

1980   Johnny Logan won the Eurovision Song Contest for Ireland with **What's Another Year** and was No 1 in the UK charts for two weeks in May. He won again in 1987 with **Hold Me Now**.
Abba had their first No 1 of the year with **Winner Takes it All** followed in November with **Super Trouper.**

1981   Two singles stayed at the top of the charts for 5 weeks each this year. First Adam and the Ants with **Stand and Deliver** and in December, The Human League with **Don't You Want Me** which was also the best-selling single of the year.

1982   The year's best seller was Dexey's Midnight Runners and **Come on Eileen**, their second No 1 in the UK. The words express the feelings of an adolescent dreaming of being free from the strictures of a Catholic society and sounded unlike the other hits of the era, no synthesiser, but a banjo, accordion, fiddle and saxophone.

1983   **Karma Chameleon** by the 'New Romantic' band, Culture Club, fronted by singer Boy George, whose androgynous style of dressing caught the attention of the public and the media, became the second Culture Club single to reach No 1 and stayed there for six weeks, also becoming the best-selling single of the year.

1984 Two Tribes, the anti-war song by the Liverpool band, Frankie Goes to Hollywood, was a phenomenal success helped by a wide range of remixes and supported by an advertising campaign depicting the band as members of the Red Army. It entered the charts at No 1 and stayed there for nine consecutive weeks, making it the the longest-running No 1 single of the decade.

1985 - 1989

1985   The best seller this year was **The Power of Love** sung by Jennifer Rush. No 1 for five weeks, Rush became the first female artist ever to have a million-selling single in the UK.
Wham and George Michael, having had three No 1's last year, **Wake Me Up Before You Go-Go, Careless Whisper** and **Freedom**, managed only one this year, **I'm Your Man.**

1986   Holiday disco songs such as **Agadoo**, topped the charts for three weeks.
The Christmas No 1 spot was held for four weeks by a reissue, three years after his death, of Jackie Wilson's **Reet Petite (The Sweetest Girl in Town)**.

1987   Two singles stayed at No 1 for five weeks, the best-selling of the year, **Never Gonna Give You Up** by Rick Astley and **China in Your Hand** by T'Pau, Carol Decker's group named after the character in Star Trek.

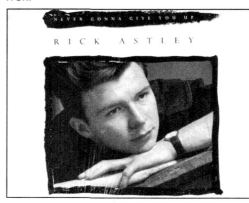

1988   Already known from the Australian soap opera, 'Neighbours', Kylie Minogue burst into the UK charts with **I Should Be So Lucky** from her debut studio album. The song became a worldwide hit.
Cliff Richard was back at No 1 after quite a break, with **Mistletoe and Wine** for the Christmas market.

1989   It was a good year for the Australian golden couple, Jason Donovan and Kylie Minogue. One No 1 together, **Especially For You,** two for Jason, **Too Many Broken Hearts** and **Sealed With a Kiss**, and one for Kylie, **Hand on Your Heart.**
Ride on Time from the debut album by Italian house music group, Black Box, topped the charts for six weeks and sold the most copies of the year.

Charity Fund Raisers

The 80's saw many 'not for profit' Charity Singles, the best-known being Bob Geldorf and Midge Ure's 'Band Aid' and then 'Live Aid', formed to raise money for famine relief in Ethiopia, who released **Do They Know Its Christmas**, for the first time, in December 1984. It stayed at the top of the charts for five weeks and was the best-selling record of the decade having been released again in 1989.

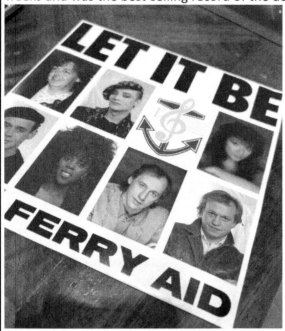

A less well-known charity, 'Ferry Aid', recorded the Beatles' song, **Let It Be** in 1987. This followed the sinking of the ferry 'Ms Herald of the Free' at Zeebrugge, killing 193 passengers and crew. The recording was organised by The Sun newspaper, after it had sold cheap tickets for the ferry on that day.

Tears For Fears, Duran Duran and Simple Minds got together and released **Everybody Wants to Rule the World** in 1986 in support of 'Sport Aid', a campaign to help tackle famine in Africa.

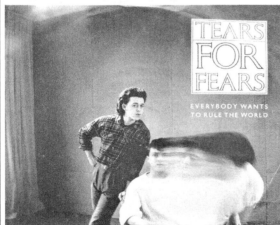

In 1983, Michael Jackson redefined the style, course, and possibilities of music videos. He released **Thriller** and made recording history. The album spent thirty-seven weeks at No 1 on the US Billboard chart. By early 1984, thirty million copies had been sold, and it was still selling at a rate of more than a million copies a week worldwide.

The Compact Disc

In 1981, Kieran Prendiville on BBC's 'Tomorrow's World', demonstrated the CD and wondered, "Whether or not there is a market for these discs, remains to be seen." Well, on the 25th anniversary of its first public release in 1982, it was estimated that 200 billion CDs had been sold worldwide so I guess the answer was "Yes"!

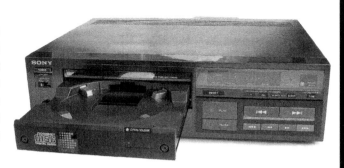

At the end of the 70's, Philips and Sony had teamed up to begin working on CDs for the public and decided on a thin, shiny and circular storage disc, which could hold about 80 minutes of music. The disc had a diameter of 120mm, Sony having insisted that the longest musical performance, Beethoven's entire 9th Symphony at 74 minutes, should fit. A CD could hold an immense amount of data, much more than the vinyl record or the cassette and was perfectly portable.

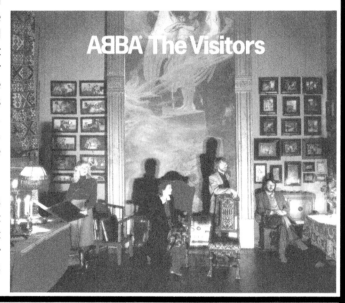

The first commercial CD to be pressed was **Visitors** by Abba, followed quickly by the first album, Billy Joel's **52nd Street**. The biggest selling CD of all time is the Eagles 1976 **Their Greatest Hits** album, which has sold over 38 million copies.

UFOs in the Forest

On 26 December 1980, several US Airforce personnel stationed near the east gate at RAF Woodbridge, reported they had seen "lights" apparently descending into nearby Rendlesham Forest. They initially thought it was a downed aircraft but, upon investigation, they saw what they described as a glowing object, metallic in appearance, with coloured lights.

After daybreak on the morning of December 27, servicemen returned to a small clearing in the forest and found three small impressions on the ground in a triangular pattern, as well as burn marks and broken branches on nearby trees.

The 'Rendlesham Forest Incident' made headline news and theories suggest it was either an actual alien visitation, a secret military aircraft, a misinterpretation of natural lights, the beam of Orfordness Lighthouse, or just a hoax.

IN THE 1980s

Mount St Helens

In March 1980 a series of volcanic explosions began at Mount St Helens, Washington in the US, culminating in a major explosive eruption on May 18. The eruption column rose 80,000 feet (15 miles) into the atmosphere and deposited ash over 11 states and into some Canadian provinces. At the same time, snow, ice, and entire glaciers on the volcano melted, forming a series of large volcanic mudslides that reached as far as 50 miles to the southwest. Thermal energy released during the eruption was equal to 26 megatons of TNT.

Regarded as the most significant and disastrous volcanic eruption in the country's history, about 57 people were killed, hundreds of square miles were reduced to wasteland, thousands of animals were killed, and Mount St. Helens was left with a crater on its north side. The area is now preserved as the Mount St Helens National Volcanic Monument.

One day before the eruption and several months afterwards. About a third of the mountain was blown away.

SPORT

1980 - 1984

1980 Eight days after the **Boston marathon**, Rosie Ruiz, a Cuban American, is disqualified as the winner 'in the fastest time ever run by a woman'. Investigations found that she did not run the entire course, joining about a half-mile before the finish.

Larry Holmes defeats Muhammed Ali to retain boxing's **WBC World Heavyweight** title. It is Ali's last world title bout.

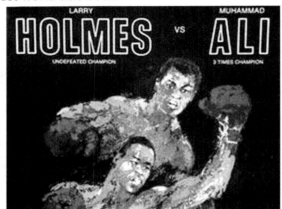

1981 At **Wimbledon**, John McEnroe defeats Björn Borg to gain his 3rd career Grand Slam title and his 1st Wimbledon title.

In the ladies' final, Chris Evert Lloyd defeats Hana Mandlíková to gain her 12th career Grand Slam title and her third and last Wimbledon title.

1982 In June, at Pebble Beach, the American Tom Watson wins **The US Open** and a month later, at Royal Troon, he wins the **The Open.** He is only the third golfer, at that time, to win both Championships in the same year.

In Spain, Italy defeat West Germany in the **World Cup Final.** The tournament features the first penalty shoot-out in the World Cup competition.

1983 The **FA Cup** is won by Manchester United who, having drawn the first final with Brighton and Hove Albion, win the replay, 4-0.

1984 John McEnroe has his best season. He wins 13 singles tournaments, including **Wimbledon** where he loses just one set on his way to his third Wimbledon singles title. This includes a straight set win over Jimmy Connors in the final. He also wins the **US Open**, capturing the year-end number one ranking.

1985 - 1989

1985 Ireland is the championship winner in the **Rugby Five Nations** winning their tenth solo title, but it would prove to be their last for 24 years, until their Grand Slam in 2009.

Alain Prost becomes the **F1 World Champion** Driver, winning five of the sixteen Grand Prix. The first ever world championship **Australian Grand Prix** is held on a street circuit in Adelaide.

1986 In the **World Cup**, Argentina wins by defeating West Germany 3-2. Diego Maradona is the biggest star of the event, and his 'Hand of God' goal is well remembered. The event also sees the introduction of the 'Mexican Wave'.

1987 In **Cricket** the Indian opening batsman, Sunil Gavaskar reaches 10,000 test runs to become the first ever player to score this many. In the **Cricket World Cup** played for the first time outside Britain, in India, Australia win by defeating their arch-rivals, England.

1988 The **FA Cup** is won by Wimbledon FC's 'Crazy Gang', who defeat league champions Liverpool through a headed goal by Lawrie Sanchez. This is Wimbledon's only FA Cup title during its lifetime.

1989 On heavy, almost un-raceable ground, the iconic grey Desert Orchid, ridden by Simon Sherwood, in a race that defined his illustrious career, wins the **Cheltenham Gold Cup.** In 2005 this was voted the 'Greatest Race of All Time' by Racing Post readers.

You cannot be serious!

During the 1981 Wimbledon Championships, John McEnroe uttered what has become the most immortal phrase in tennis, if not all sport, when he screamed "you cannot be serious" at a Wimbledon umpire while disputing a line call. Already called "Superbrat" by the British tabloid press for his verbal volleys during previous Wimbledon matches, it was in a first-round match against fellow American Tom Gullikson, who was serving at 15-30 and 1-1 in the first set when a McEnroe shot was called out. Approaching the umpire, he said: "Chalk came up all over the place, you can't be serious man." Then, his anger rising, he bawled the words that would stay with him for a lifetime and find its way into the sporting annals. "You cannot be serious," he screamed. "That ball was on the line".

On the receiving end of the tirade was umpire Edward James, who eventually responded by politely announcing: "I'm going to award a point against you Mr McEnroe." It made little difference, McEnroe went on to win in straight sets and two weeks later had his final victory over Bjorn Borg.

Torvill and Dean

On Valentine's Day 1984, Jayne Torvill and Christopher Dean made history at the Winter Olympics in Sarajevo and set a new standard for world class figure skating. The duo from Nottingham, were the last to perform in their category and their performance, self-choreographed to 4½ minutes of Ravel's Bolero, was seamless, elegant and hypnotic. As they sank to the ice in the dramatic finale, the whole stadium stood and applauded. Their dance had captured the world's imagination and won Gold. The unanimous scores of 6.0 for artistic impression made them the highest-scoring figure skaters of all time.

Their routine, made Ravel's Boléro with its steady crescendo and repeated snare-drum rhythms, synonymous with figure-skating.

British Car Manufacturing

Gallery:

The 1980s was still a busy period for British car manufacturers and many of the bestselling cars of the decade were made in Britain.

The top 10 cars were:

1. Ford Escort
2. Vauxhall Cavalier
3. Ford Fiesta
4. Austin Metro
5. Ford Sierra (which replaced the
6. Ford Cortina)
6. Vauxhall Astra
7. Ford Orion
8. Austin Maestro
9. Vauxhall Nova
10. Ford Grenada

However the list of the **'Most influential Cars of the 1980s'** shows how the British car industry was soon to be decimated. The list includes:

Audi Quatrro; Porsche 944: Renault Scenic; Mercedes 190; BMW 3 Series; VW Golf; Volvo 240 Estate; Peugeot 205 and the Toyota Carolla.

The Ford Cortina was replaced by the Ford Sierra in 1982

The Ford Fiesta has been ever popular right up to the present day.

The Austin Metro was the replacement for the mini.

The VW Golf had front wheel drive and built a reputation for quality and reliability

The Porsche 944 was the choice of the newly rich 'yuppies' of the 1980s

---

Clunk Click Every Trip

Although car manufacturers had been obliged to install seatbelts since 1965, it was not until January 1983 that the law requiring all drivers to wear their belts came into force. In spite of a great deal of 'grumbling' and more, ranging from *"the erosion of our civil liberties, another example of the Nanny State",* to *"its uncomfortable, restrictive and creases my clothes"* and horror stories of crash victims being *"hanged"* by their belts or suffering greater injury, 90% of drivers and front seat passengers were observed to be wearing seat belts soon after the law came into effect – and these rates have been sustained since then. There was an immediate 25% reduction in driver fatalities and a 29 per cent reduction in fatal injuries among front seat passengers.

In 1989 it became compulsory for all children under 14 to wear a seat belt in the rear and when seatbelt wearing became compulsory for all rear-seat occupants in 1991, there was an immediate increase from 10% to 40% in observed seat belt wearing rates.

Aviation

When Airbus designed the A300 during the late 1960s and early 1970s, it envisaged a broad family of airliners with which to compete against Boeing and Douglas, the two established US aerospace manufacturers.

The launch of the A320 in 1987 guaranteed the status of Airbus as a major player in the aircraft market – the aircraft had over 400 orders before it first flew.

Motorcycles

Only 3000 Honda FVR750R motorcycles were made, race bred machines with lights thrown on to make them road legal and sold to the public. The first batch of 1000 sold out instantly. With a top speed of 153mph the V-four powered RC30 was one of the fastest sports bike of the decade but it was the track proven frame that meant it handled like a genuine racer. It also had a soundtrack to die for and was absolutely beautiful.

The Docklands Light Railway

The Docklands Light Railway was first opened in August 1987 as an automated, light metro system to serve the redeveloped Docklands area of London as a cheap public transport solution. The original network comprised two routes - Tower Gateway to Island Gardens and Stratford to Island Gardens and was mainly elevated on disused railway viaducts, new concrete viaducts and disused surface railway tracks. The trains were fully automated, controlled by computer, and had no driver.

They did however have a "Train Captain" who was responsible for patrolling the train, checking tickets, making announcements and controlling the doors. They could take control of the train should there be an equipment failure or emergency. The first generation of rolling stock comprised eleven lightweight units and the stations, mostly of a common design, constructed from standard components and usually featuring a short half-cylindrical, glazed, blue canopy, were designed specifically for these single articulated trains. The 15 stations were all above ground and needed no staff.

1990 - 1994

1990:
Feb: Nelson Mandela is released from prison in South Africa, after 27 years behind bars.

Nov: Margaret Thatcher resigns as Prime Minister. At 11 years, she was the longest serving PM of the 20th Century.

1991:
Jan: The Gulf War begins, as the Royal Air Force joins Allied aircraft in bombing raids on Iraq

Apr: After a year of protests and riots, the government confirms that the Poll Tax is to be replaced by a new Council Tax in 1993.

1992:
Apr: At the General Election the Conservative Party are re-elected for a fourth term under John Major.

Nov: Part of Windsor Castle is gutted in a fire causing millions of pounds worth of damage and The Queen describes this year as an Annus Horribilis.

1993:
Apr: The Queen announces that Buckingham Palace will open to the public for the first time

Sep: The UK Independence Party which supports the breakaway from the EU is formed.

Dec: Diana, Princess of Wales. withdraws from public life.

1994:
Mar: The Church of England ordains its first female priests.

May: The Channel Tunnel between Britain and France is officially opened.

Nov: The first UK National Lottery draw takes place.

1992: The 'Maastricht Treaty' was concluded between the 'then' twelve member states of the European Communities. This foundation treaty of the EU announced a new stage in the process of European integration, shared citizenship and a single currency. There were two headquarters, one in Brussels and one in Strasbourg,

1991: The internet already existed but no one had thought of a way of how to link one document directly to another until in 1989, British scientist Tim Berners-Lee, invented the WorldWideWeb. The www. was introduced in 1991 as the first web browser and the first website went online in August.

1995 - 1999

1997: The UK transfers sovereignty of Hong Kong, the largest remaining British colony, to the People's Republic of China as the 99 years lease on the territory formally ends.

1999: On 1st January, the new European currency, the Euro is launched and some 320 million people from eleven European countries begin carrying the same money in their wallets.
Britain's Labour government preferred to stay with the pound sterling instead.

1995:
Feb: Barings Bank, the UK's oldest merchant bank, collapses after rogue trader Nick Leeson loses $1.4 billion.

Apr: All telephone area dialling codes are changed in the UK.

Aug: Pubs in England are permitted to remain open throughout Sunday afternoon.

1996:
Feb: The Prince and Princess of Wales agree to divorce more than three years after separating.

Jul: Dolly the Sheep becomes the first mammal to be successfully cloned from an adult cell.

1997:
May: Tony Blair wins a landslide General Election for the Labour Party.

Aug: Princess Diana is killed in a car crash in Paris. Dodi Fayed, the heir to the Harrods empire is killed with her

1998:
Mar: Construction on the Millenium Dome begins. It will be the centre piece for a national celebration.

Apr: The Good Friday Agreement between the UK and Irish governments is signed.

1999:
Apr: A minimum wage is introduced in the UK – set at £3.60 an hour for workers over 21, and £3 for workers under 21

Jun: Construction of the Millenium Dome is finished and in October, the London Eye begins to be lifted into position.

THE HOME

Home life in the 1990s was changing again. Family time was not cherished as it had once been, children had a lot more choice and were becoming more independent with their own TVs programmes, personal computers, music systems, mobile phones and, crucially, the introduction of the world wide web, which meant life would never be the same again.

After school and weekend organised activities for the young burgeoned, with teenagers able to take advantage of the fast-food chains, or eating at different times, meaning no more family eating together. Families 'lived in separate' rooms, there were often two televisions so different channels could be watched and children wanted to play with their Nintendos or listen to their Walkmans in their own rooms. Their rooms were increasingly themed, from Toy Story to Athena posters, a ceiling full of sticker stars that illuminated a room with their green glow and somewhere in the house, room had to be made for the computer desk.

Track lighting was an easy way to illuminate a room without relying on multiple lamps and it became a popular feature in many '90s homes along with corner baths — most of which also had a water jet function which suddenly turned your bath into a low-budget jacuzzi!

In 1990, 68% of UK households owned at least one car, and the use of 'out of town' supermarkets and shopping centres, where just about anything and everything could be purchased in the same area, meant that large weekly or even monthly shops could be done in a single outing and combined with the huge increase in domestic freezers and ready prepared foods, time spent in the kitchen and cooking could be greatly reduced.

Over 80% of households owned a washing machine and 50%, a tumble dryer, so the need to visit the laundrette all but disappeared and instead of "Monday is washing day", the family's laundry could be carried out on an 'as and when' basis. All contributing to an increase in leisure time.

merry maids
Relax. It's Done.

Nearly three-quarters of homes had microwave cookers and for working women who did not want to do their own cleaning, Merry Maids set up their home cleaning franchise in the UK in 1990 and many other companies followed suit.

Commuting

In Great Britain at the beginning of the 1990s, the *average* one-way commute to work was 38 minutes in London, 33 minutes in the south-east, and 21 minutes in the rest of the country. By the end of the decade, full-time workers commuting to and from London, had lost an additional 70 minutes per week of home time to commuting but, by contrast, outside the south-east of Britain, there was no increase in commuting time over the decade. In the south-east, 30% of workers took at least 45 minutes to get to work. In the rest of the country, only 10% did.

ART AND CULTURE

1990 - 1994

1990 In Rome, on the eve of the final of the FIFA World Cup, the Three Tenors sing together for the first time. The event is broadcast live and watched worldwide by millions of people. The highlight is Luciano Pavarotti's performance of Nessun Dorma.
The first Hampton Court Palace Flower Show takes place.

1991 Dame Margot Fonteyn, the Royal Ballet's Prima Ballerina, dies in Panama City, exactly 29 years after her premiere with Rudolf Nureyev who made his debut in 'Giselle'.

1992 Damien Hirst's "Shark", featuring a preserved shark, is first shown at an exhibition at the Saatchi Gallery in London.
Under the new Further and Higher Education Act, Polytechnics are allowed to become new Universities and award degrees of their own.
The last edition of Punch, the UK's oldest satirical magazine since 1841, is published.

1993 Bookmakers cut their odds on the monarchy being abolished by the year 2000 from 100 to 1 to 50 to 1.
QVC launches the first television shopping channel in the UK.

1994 The Duchess of Kent joins the Roman Catholic Church, the first member of the Royal Family to convert to Catholicism for more than 300 years.
The Sunday Trading Act comes into full effect, permitting retailers to trade on Sundays but restricts larger stores to a maximum of six hours, between 10 am and 6 pm.

1995 - 1999

1995 The first ever World Book Day was held on 23rd April, picked to celebrate the anniversary of William Shakespeare's death.

The BBC begins regular Digital Audio Broadcasting from Crystal Palace.

1996 Shortly after publication of the Italian edition of his book 'The Art Forger's Handbook', English-born art forger, Eric Hebborn is beaten to death in Rome.
The Stone of Scone is installed in Edinburgh Castle 700 years after it was removed from Scotland by King Edward I of England.

1997 The Teletubbies caused a sensation when they appeared on BBC TV. They were the most sought-after toy of the year.
The reconstruction of the Elizabethan Globe Theatre, called Shakespeare's Globe opens in London with a production of Shakespeare's 'Henry V'.

1998 Britain's largest sculpture, the Angel of the North by Anthony Gormley is installed at Low Eighton, Gateshead.
More than 15,000 people attend a tribute concert held for Diana, Princess of Wales, at her family home, Althorp Park.

1999 The children's picture book, 'The Gruffalo' by Julia Donaldson is first published.

Media coverage for the Turner Prize was dominated by extreme critical response to Tracey Emin's work 'My Bed' – an installation of her unmade bed, complete with dirty sheets and detritus.

IN THE 1990s

1997: 'Harry Potter and the Philosopher's Stone' by JK Rowling made its debut in June. The initial edition of this first book in the series, comprised 500 copies and the novel has gone on to sell in excess of 120 million. The success of the whole Harry Potter phenomenon is well known, and there have been less expected benefits too. Certainly, before the films, children loved reading the books and boosted the reported numbers of children reading and indeed, reading longer books.

The perception of boarding schools, often associated with misery and cruel, spartan regimes was changed for some by Hogwarts School of Witchcraft and Wizardry. The sense of excitement, community and friendship of the children, the camaraderie of eating together and playing together, made going away to school more appealing for many.

The amazing visual effects used in the films were instrumental in persuading Hollywood to consider UK technical studios and raised the number of visual effects Oscar nominations for British companies significantly.

1997: The Guggenheim Museum of modern and contemporary art, designed by Canadian-American architect Frank Gehry, opened in Bilbao. The building represents an architectural landmark of innovating design, a spectacular structure.

The museum was originally a controversial project. Bilbao's industry, steel and shipbuilding was dying, and the city decided to regenerate to become a modern technological hub of the Basque region, and the controversy was, instead of an office block or factory, the centre piece would be a brand-new art gallery.

It is a spectacular building, more like a sculpture with twisted metal, glass, titanium and limestone, a futuristic setting for fine works of art. The gamble paid off, in the first twenty years, the museum attracted more than 19 million visitors with 70% from outside Spain. Foreign tourists continue to travel through the Basque country bringing a great economic boost to the region and Bilbao itself, has transformed from a grimy post-industrial town to a tourist hotspot.

FILMS

1990 - 1994

1990 It was Oscar time for an epic western this year and **Dances With Wolves**, directed and starring Kevin Costner with seven Academy Awards, won Best Picture and Best Director. It is one of only three Westerns to win the Oscar for Best Picture, the other two being **Cimmaron** in 1931 and **Unforgotten** in **1992**.

1991 *"Well, Clarice - have the lambs stopped screaming?"* wrote Dr Hannibal Lecter to the young FBI trainee, Clarice Starling. The thriller, **The Silence of the Lambs**, about a cannibalistic serial killer, scared audiences half to death and won the Best Picture Award.

1992 The nominations for the Academy Awards held some serious themes. **The Crying Game** was set against the backdrop of the 'troubles' in Northern Ireland. There was a blind retired Army officer in **Scent of a Woman**, rising troubles in colonial French Vietnam in **Indochine** and the invasion of Panama in **The Panama Deception**.

1993 The acclaimed **Schindler's List** won Best Picture with stiff competition from **The Piano** which won Best Original Screenplay and Robin Williams as **Mrs Doubtfire** which became the second highest grossing film of the year.

1994 Disney's animated musical **The Lion King** made the most money this year, but **Forest Gump** took the prize for Best Picture. The British film **Four Weddings and a Funeral** was a huge success and brought WH Auden's beautiful poem 'Funeral Blues' into the limelight.

1995 - 1999

1995 The tense, amazingly technically correct, story of the ill-fated **Apollo 13** quest to land on the moon failed to win the top Oscar, beaten by Mel Gibson in **Braveheart**, the American take on the story of William Wallace and the first Scottish war of independence against England.

1996 The English Patient a romantic war drama won the Best Picture, up against Mike Leigh's **Secrets and Lies** which won the Best British Film.

1997 The blockbuster **Titanic** was the film of the year. The combination of romance and disaster proving irresistible. Harland & Wolfe, the builders of RMS Titanic shared blueprints they thought were lost with the crew to produce the scale models, computer-generated imagery and a reconstruction of the ship itself, to re-create the sinking.

1998 Shakespeare in Love, a fictional love affair between Shakespeare and Viola de Lesseps whilst he is writing Romeo and Juliet was hugely popular and won seven Oscars.

1999 In **American Beauty,** Kevin Spacey plays Lester Burnham, an unhappy executive whose midlife awakening is the crux of the story. Bad as he thinks his life is, he cannot not stop seeing the beauty of the world around him.

**"Fear can hold you prisoner,
Hope can set you free."**

In 1994, Tim Robbins and Morgan Freeman starred **The Shawshank Redemption**, an inspirational, life-affirming and uplifting, old-fashioned style prison film and character study in the ilk of 'The Birdman of Alcatraz'. Set in a fictional, oppressive Shawshank State Prison in Maine, two imprisoned men bond over the years, in a tale of friendship, patience, hope, survival and ultimately finding solace and eventual redemption through acts of common decency.

The film was initially a box office disappointment. Many reasons were put forward for its failure at the time, including a general unpopularity of prison films, its lack of female characters and even the title, which was considered to be confusing. However, it was nominated for seven Academy Awards, failed to win a single Oscar, but this raised awareness and increased the film's popularity such that it is now preserved in the US National Film Registry as "culturally, historically, or aesthetically significant".

The Full Monty

Six men. With nothing to lose. Who dared to go...

THE YEAR'S MOST REVEALING COMEDY.

In 1997 whilst huge audiences were crying over Kate Winslet and Leonardo di Caprio in **Titanic,** equally huge audiences were laughing at the story of six unemployed men in Sheffield, four of them former steel workers, who are in dire need of cash and who decide to emulate 'The Chippendales' dance, striptease troupe. They devise a dance act with their difference being, that Gaz decides their show must be even better than the originals and declares to the friends that they will go 'the full Monty' – they will strip all the way. Although primarily a comedy, the film touches on several serious subjects too, including unemployment, father's rights – Gaz is unable to pay maintenance to his estranged wife and she is seeking sole custody of his son – and working-class culture, depression and suicide. The film was a huge success as it ultimately is about humanity and the problems people all over the world struggle with.

FASHION

SUPERMODELS

The original supermodels of the 1980s, Linda Evangelista, Naomi Campbell, Christy Turlington and Cindy Crawford were joined later by Claudia Schiffer and then Kate Moss to become the "Big Six". Models used to be categorised as 'print' or 'runway' but the "Big Six" showed that they could do it all, catwalk, print campaigns, magazine covers and even music videos and they became pop 'icons' in their own right. The models were also known for their earning capacity, one famous remark from Linda Evangelista, "We don't wake up for less than $10,000 a day!"

But with the popularity of grunge, came a shift away from the fashion for feminine curves and wholesome looking women, and in came the rise of a new breed of fragile, individual-looking and often younger, models, epitomised by Kate Moss. Her waif-like thinness and delicacy complemented the unkempt look that was popular in the early nineties and a new phrase 'heroin chic' described the down-at-heel settings for fashion shoots presented in magazines. By the end of the decade however, attitudes had shifted and concern about the health of the skeletal model was becoming a source of great debate.

GOTH

During the mid to late 1990s, the sub-culture of gothic fashion peaked in popularity. Their distinguishing features were black, antiquated and homogeneous features. Long black hair, black eyeliner, black nail polish, silver jewellery and face piercings teamed with long, black leather coats worn over frilly shirts and tight black trousers or even fetish wear. Girls often wore corsets, lace gloves and short leather skirts, velvets and fishnets with accessories often borrowed from the punk fashion such as spiked wristbands and chokers.

Siouxsie Sioux was particularly influential, since her gig at Futurama in 1980 she had been influencing how the music with the Banshees, would dress and she may well have been inspired by Theda Bara, the 1910s silent film, femme fatale, renowned for her dark eyeshadow and 'Vamp' look.

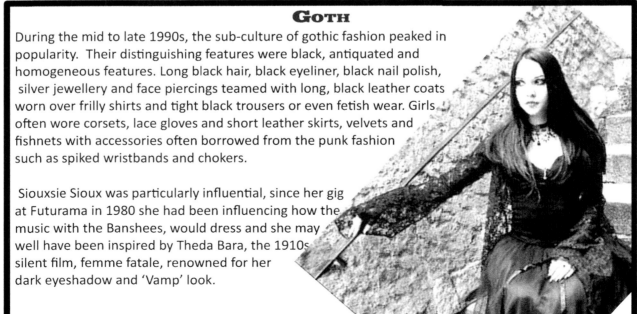

GRUNGE

Grunge was a style for the young that emerged in Seattle in the late 1980s and by the early 90s had spread across the world. Made popular by bands such as Nirvana, it was a fashion for both men and women. The look was simple, an oversized flannel shirt, sometimes worn over a t-shirt, and baggy, worn out jeans to give an overall, dishevelled, appearance. The clothes were found ideally in charity shops or at the back of "Dad's wardrobe". A pair of Doc Martens or Converse shoes finished the ensemble.

Nirvana's lead singer Kurt Cobain epitomised the look with holes in his jeans and cardigan sweaters and the fashion world caught on when their second album, 'Nevermind' was released in 1991 and grunge made it onto the catwalk — specifically by Calvin Klein on an 18-year-old Kate Moss. Shrunken baby doll dresses, old prom dresses or even old petticoats and simple slip dresses appeared, often worn with chunky boots and for men, beanies, band t-shirts and knitted sweaters with patterns.

FRIENDS

For women, long loose hair was the most popular women's style, but the most requested hairstyle of the 1990s was said to be 'The Rachel'. Jennifer Anniston's character in 'Friends', Rachel Green, had the haircut people wanted — bouncy, layered, shoulder length, obviously styled to within an inch of its life yet at the same time artfully tousled.

HOODIES

Utilitarian styles such as cargo pants and The Gap's hooded sweatshirts became popular for everyday wear. Industrial and military styles crept into mainstream fashion and camouflage pants were everywhere on the street.

There was also a concerted move towards logoed clothing such as by Tommy Hilfiger

LEISURE

THE GAMES CHILDREN PLAYED

The trend in the 90s was for more electronic, video and computer games but younger children still enjoyed many of the traditional past-times, and events in the 90s such as the FIFA World Cups and the Olympics, produced special collections which reignited interest in collecting 'stickers,' and filling albums.

Crazes were still all the craze too and it was digital pets like Tamagotchi, housed in their small, egg-shaped, handheld video game console that became the biggest fads of the end of the decade.

The Teletubbies caused a huge sensation in 1997, communicating through gibberish and designed to resemble real-life toddlers, they became a huge commercial success, the toy Teletubbies being the most demanded toy of 1997.

However, it was Sony's PlayStation which was the big innovation of the 90s. The first version was able to process games stored on CD-ROMs and introduced 3D graphics to the industry. It had a low retail price and Sony employed aggressive youth marketing. Ridge Racer was the classic motor racing game used in the launch and the popularity of this game was crucial to the early success of the PlayStation.

RESTORATION OF THE SPA

From being at the centre of society in previous times, the spa industry had declined so much that by the 50s, leading spas such as those at Buxton, Cheltenham and Tunbridge Wells had closed. The 1990s saw a simultaneous rise of increasing disposable wealth, and the popularity of a new concept of the spa, pure self-indulgence and pampering.

The need to pause and detox from time to time fitted nicely into the growth of a 'wellness' culture and the understanding of holistic wellbeing, treatments to soothe the mind, body and spirit. Wearing a luxurious white robe and slippers, lounging by a heated pool reading magazines and dipping from time to time into the whirlpools, a trip to the steam room or sauna before taking a light lunch and then unwinding to a fragranced oil body massage because, as L'Oreal had been saying since the 70s, "you're worth it!"

Where We Went on Holiday

In the 90s, if we went on a foreign holiday at all, 26m of us in 1996, the norm was to go for just the one, two-week summer break. Booking with a Travel Agent in town or finding a cheap package deal on Teletext, we arrived at our destination with a guide-book, Travellers Cheques and a camera complete with film.

Our favourite places were Spain and France, many of us travelling on the cross-Channel ferries rather than on the budget airlines. Our other favourite hot spots were Belgium, Turkey, Egypt, Kenya and Tunisia.

Although the gap year began in the 1960s, it was in the 1990s when the idea became the 'thing to do' amongst the children of the new wealthy middle classes.

Many visited India, Pakistan and Nepal, Australia, Thailand, the USA and New Zealand being their favoured countries to visit.

Some did voluntary work in the developing nations, building schools and teaching children English.

The 90s saw plenty of new cruise ships being launched for what became a massive growth industry. New cruise lines were formed, and many existing lines merged and Royal Caribbean, Celebrity, Fred Olsen and Carnival, Disney, Silver Sea and Princess lines were all introducing, predominantly older people, to new places and entertaining them royally on the way.

For others, at the opposite end of the cruising scale, was the immensely popular, 'Booze Cruise'. The day trip across the channel to France to stock up on duty free wine and cigarettes.

MUSIC

1990 - 1994

1990 Elton John's **Sacrifice** was initially released as a single in 1989 but only reached No. 55 in the UK. In mid-1990, Radio 1 DJ, Steve Wright began playing it and it soon caught on with other DJs and when re-released as a double A-side single with **Healing Hands** it became John's first solo No 1 single remaining at the top for five weeks.

1991 Cher made the 1960s **Shoop Shoop Song (It's in His Kiss)** an international hit once again. **(Everything I Do) I Do It for You**, from the soundtrack of the film 'Robin Hood: Prince of Thieves' was sung by Bryan Adams and became a huge hit, the best-selling single of the year and stayed at No 1 for 16 weeks.

1992 Shakespeares Sister had their only No 1 UK single hit with **Stay** which stayed at the top for eight consecutive weeks.
The best-selling single of the year was Whitney Houston singing the song written by Dolly Parton, **I Will Always Love You.**

1993 **Pray** by Take That, written by Gary Barlow, was the first of twelve singles by the band to reach No 1 in the UK and the first of a run of four consecutive No 1's.

I'd Do Anything for Love (But I Won't Do That) was the song of the year and won Meat Loaf a Grammy Award for the Best Rock Solo Vocal Performance.

1994 The Most Beautiful Girl in the World by the unpronounceable Love Symbol, or 'The Artist Formerly Known as Prince' reached No 1.
The Manchester United football squad had the help of Status Quo, who wrote and sang along on their two week No 1 hit, **Come on You Reds.**

1995 - 1999

1995 Four artists had two No 1 hits this year. The Outhere Brothers with **Don't Stop (Wiggle Wiggle)** and **Boom Boom Boom**. Take That with **Back for Good** and **Never Forget** and Robson Green & Jerome Flynn with **Unchained Melody/ Bluebirds Over the White Cliffs of Dover** – the best seller of the year, and **I Believe/Up On the Roof.**

1996 This was a year with 23 No 1s. Most being at the top for only one week, but Fugees was No 1 twice with the same song **Killing Me Softly.** Firstly, for four weeks in June and then with a break for a week for **Three Lions (Football's Coming Home)** and another week in July.

1997 Elton John topped the charts for five weeks with **Candle in the Wind 1997**, a re-written and re-recorded version of **Candle in the Wind** as a tribute to the late Diana, Princess of Wales.
Another kind of tribute, this time to the popularity of the Teletubbies, their **Teletubbies say 'Eh-oh!'** stayed at No 1 for two weeks in December.

1998 The main soundtrack song from the blockbuster film Titanic provided Celine Dion with a hit, **My Heart Will Go On.**
Cher reinvented herself, and her song, **Believe** stayed at No 1 for seven weeks and was the year's best seller.

1999 Britney Spears made her debut single with **...Baby One More Time** which became a worldwide hit and sold over ten million copies.
Cliff Richard's **Millenium Prayer** is knocked off its 3 weeks at No 1 spot just in time for the boy band, Westlife, to make the Christmas No 1 with **I Have a Dream/Seasons in the Sun.**

IN THE 1990s

COOL BRITANNIA

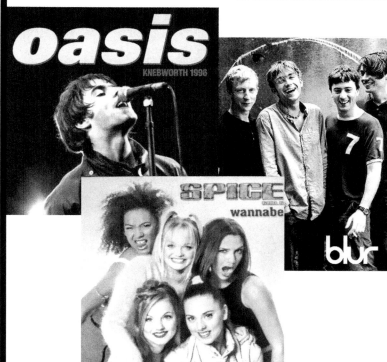

Throughout the mid and second half of the 1990s, Cool Britannia was a period of increased pride in the culture of the UK inspired by the 'Swinging London' of the 1960s pop culture. This brought about a huge success of 'Britpop' with groups such as Blur and Oasis and particularly, the Spice Girls.

Mel B, 'Scary Spice', Melanie C, 'Sporty Spice', Emma Bunton, 'Baby Spice', Geri Halliwell, 'Ginger Spice' and Victoria Beckham, 'Posh Spice' brought girl power to the fore. Their first single was 1996's iconic **Wannabe**, which established the group as a global phenomenon as 'Spice Mania' circled the globe. They scored the Christmas Number 1 single three years in a row and had nine UK No 1's in total.

LOVE IS ALL AROUND

In June 1994, Wet Wet Wet the Scottish soft rock band had a huge international hit, with 15 weeks as the UK No 1, with their cover of the 1960s hit by The Troggs, **Love Is All Around.** Their version was used on the soundtrack of the blockbuster film 'Four Weddings and a Funeral'.

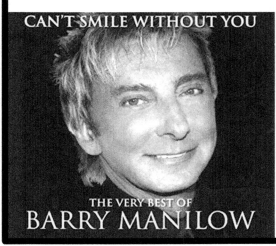

Richard Curtis, the director of the film, had approached Wet Wet Wet with a choice of three cover songs to record for the soundtrack, the other two being **I Will Survive** by Gloria Gaynor and Barry Manilow's **Can't Smile Without You**.

SCIENCE AND NATURE

THE HUBBLE TELESCOPE

The Hubble telescope is a general-purpose orbiting observatory. Orbiting approximately 380 mi (612 km) above Earth, the 12.5-ton Hubble Space Telescope has peered farther into the universe than any telescope before it. The Hubble, which was launched on April 24, 1990, has produced images with unprecedented resolution at visible, near-ultraviolet, and near-infrared wavelengths since its originally faulty optics were corrected in 1993.

Although ground-based telescopes are finally starting to catch up, the Hubble continues to produce a stream of unique observations. During the 1990s and now into the 2000s, the Hubble has revolutionised the science of astronomy, becoming one, if not the most, important instruments ever used in astronomy.

ADD TO BASKET

Mint Velvet Star Print Jumper, Pink

£69.00

Free Click & Collect over £30 & free returns
View delivery & returns options

Size: size guide

XS   S   M   L

XL

Add to your basket

♡ Add to wish list

ROYAL ALBERT OLD COUNTRY ROSES 40 PIECE DINNER TEA SET SERVICE TEASET ENGLAND

Condition: Used

Time left: 32m 7s | 01 Mar 2022 12:35:54 GMT

Current bid: **£185.00** [32 bids]

Bid amount

Submit bid

Enter £190.00 or more   ♡ Watch this item

Posts from United Kingdom

The first ever shopper bought online from Tesco in 1984 using her television remote control, but it was in 1990s, following the creation by Tim Berners-Lee of the World Wide Web server and browser and the commercialisation of the internet in 1991 giving birth to e-commerce, that online shopping really began to take off.

In 1995, Amazon began selling books online, computer companies started using the internet for *all* their transactions and Auction Web was set up by Pierre Omidyar as a site *"dedicated to bringing together buyers and sellers in an honest and open marketplace."* We now know this as eBay and we can buy just about anything on Amazon.

Comparison sites were set up in 1997 and in 1998, PayPal was founded, the way to pay online without having to share your financial information. By 1999, online only shops were beginning to emerge and paved the way for 'Click for Checkout' to become commonplace.

In The 1990s

The Kyoto Protocol

In December 1997, at the instigation of the United Nations, representatives from 160 countries met in Kyoto, Japan, to discuss climate change and draft the Kyoto Protocol which aimed to restrict the greenhouse gas emissions associated with global warming.

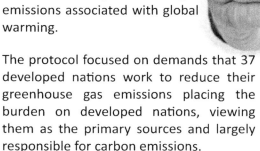

The protocol focused on demands that 37 developed nations work to reduce their greenhouse gas emissions placing the burden on developed nations, viewing them as the primary sources and largely responsible for carbon emissions.

Developing nations were asked only to comply voluntarily, exempted from the protocol's requirements. The protocol's approach included establishing a 'carbon credits system' whereby nations can earn credits by participating in emission reduction projects in other nations. A carbon credit is a tradeable permit or certificate that provides the holder

Shock Waves

A large earthquake, by British standards, occurred near Bishop's Castle, Shropshire on the Welsh Borders on 2 April 1990 at 13:46 GMT. With a magnitude of 5.1, the shock waves were felt over a wide area of Britain, from Ayrshire in the north to Cornwall in the south, Kent in the east and Dublin in the west.

Worldwide in 1990, there were 18 quakes of magnitude 7.0 or above and 134 quakes between 6.0 and 7.0, 4435 quakes between 4.0 and 5.0, 2755 quakes between 3.0 and 4.0, and 8618 quakes between 2.0 and 3.0. There were also 29800 quakes below magnitude 2.0 which people don't normally feel.

The strongest quake was north of Pulau Hulawa Island in Indonesia, registering 7.8 on the Richter scale.

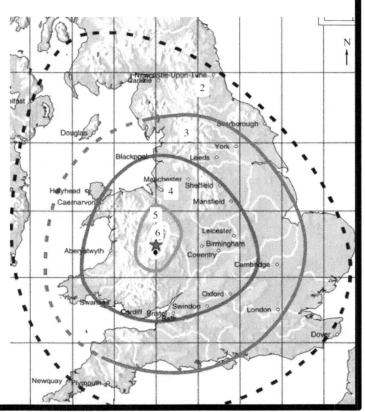

SPORT

1990 - 1994

1990 West Germany won the **FIFA World Cup** in Rome, defeating defending champions Argentina, 1–0 in the final.

The British golfer, Nick Faldo, had an amazing year, winning both the **Masters** and the Claret Jug at the **Open** at St Andrews, and capturing the PGA Player of the Year award, the first non-American to do so.

1991 At the **World Athletics** Championships in Tokyo, Mike Powell broke the 23 year-long world record **long jump** set by Bob Beamon, with a jump of 29' 4½".

1992 The rugby, **Five Nations Championship** is won by England who complete the Grand Slam for the second consecutive year.

The summer **Olympics** are held in Barcelona, Spain where Sally Gunnell takes home gold in the Women's 400 metres hurdles, Linford Christie triumphs in the Men's 100 metres, and rowers Matthew Pinsent and Steve Redgrave finish first in the Men's coxless pair, the first Olympic gold for all four athletes. In the **Paralympics**, Tanni Grey-Thompson in her debut Games, takes home four golds and a silver.

1993 Manchester United win the inaugural **English Premier League** title, their first league title in 26 years.

Shane Warne bowls the so-called 'Ball of the Century' in the first Test at Old Trafford. With his first ball against England, in his first **Ashes**, he bowled Mike Gatting out.

1994 Tiger Woods becomes the youngest man ever to win the **U.S. Amateur Golf Championships**, at age 18.

George Foreman becomes **Boxing's** oldest Heavyweight Champion at forty-five.

1995 - 1999

1995 In motor racing, Michael Schumacher wins his second consecutive **Drivers' Championship**, and Benetton wins its first and only Constructors' Championship.

British triple jumper Jonathan Edwards sets a world record in the **Athletics World Championships**, jumping 60' (18.29 m).

1996 The 95/96 **Rugby League** ends with Wigan declared champions.

Stephen Hendry wins the **World Snooker Championship** and remains the world number one.

1997 At 21, Tiger Woods becomes the youngest **Masters** winner in history, as well as the first non-white winner at Augusta. He set the scoring record at 270 and the record for the largest margin of victory at 12 strokes.

1998 In Japan, **Curling** is included in the Winter Olympics for the first time.

1999 Pete Sampras beats his biggest rival, Andre Agassi in the **Wimbledon Men's Singles** Final giving him his sixth win at the All England Club.

In the **US Open Tennis** final, at the age of 17, Serena Williams beats the number one player Martina Hingis and marks the beginning of one of the most dominant careers in the history of women's tennis.

The Dangerous Side To Sport

By 1993, Monica Seles, the Serbian-American tennis player, had won eight Grand Slam titles and was ranked No. 1 in the world. On April 30, 1993, then just 19, she was sitting on a courtside seat during a changeover in a match in Hamburg when a German man, said later to be a fan of the tennis star's German rival, Steffi Graf, leaned over a fence and stabbed her between the shoulder blades with a knife. The assailant was quickly apprehended and Seles was taken to the hospital with a wound half and inch deep in her upper back. She recovered from her physical injuries but was left with deep emotional scars and didn't play again professionally for another two years.

Leading up to the 1994 Winter Olympics, figure skater Nancy Kerrigan was attacked during a practice session. This had been 'commissioned' by the ex-husband of fellow skater, Tonya Harding and her bodyguard. Kerrigan was Harding's long-time rival and the one person in the way of her making the Olympic team, and she was desperate to win. Fortunately for Kerrigan, the injury left her with just bruises – no broken bones but she had to withdraw from the U.S. Figure Skating Championship the following night. However, she was still given a spot on the Olympic team and finished with a silver medal. Harding finished in eighth place and later had her U.S. Figure Skating Championship title revoked and was banned from the United States Figure Skating Association for life.

Also in 1994, Andrés Escobar the Colombian footballer, nicknamed 'The Gentleman' - known for his clean style of play and calmness on the pitch - was murdered following a second-round match against the US in the FIFA World Cup. This was reportedly in retaliation for Escobar having scored an own goal which contributed to the team's elimination from the tournament.

In 1997, Evander Holyfield and Mike Tyson's fight made headlines after Tyson was disqualified for biting off a part of his rival's ear, an infamous incident that would lead to the event being dubbed "The Bite Fight".

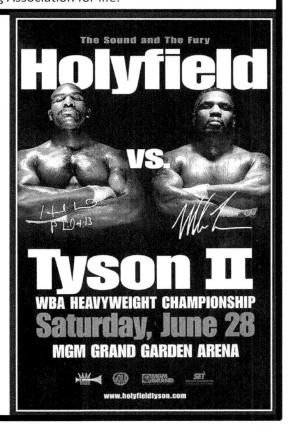

The Sound and The Fury

Holyfield

VS.

Tyson II

WBA HEAVYWEIGHT CHAMPIONSHIP

Saturday, June 28

MGM GRAND GARDEN ARENA

www.holyfieldtyson.com

TRANSPORT

HAULAGE

The 1990s was a decade devoted to environmental considerations for haulage with top priority given to cleaner emissions and low noise levels. By the end of the decade, integrated IT solutions were being used to provide the tools necessary to increase efficiency and safety.

A significant factor in the 1990s was making the lorry more aerodynamic. A 20% saving in fuel consumption meant lower emissions and also the average transport operator could improve profits by up to 50%.

CRUISE SHIPS

The largest passenger ship of the 1990s was Royal Caribbean's 'Voyager of the Seas' at 137,276 gross tonnage and 310 m (1,020 ft) long.

This record was held between Oct 1999 and Sep 2000, when it was superseded by 'Explorer of the Seas', larger by only 12 GT. Royal Caribbean have, on order, and due 2024, an Oasis class cruiser of 231,000 gross tonnage, 362 m(1,188 ft) long.

THE HIGHWAY CODE

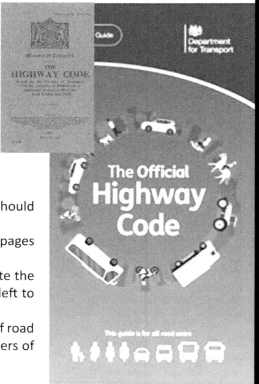

In July 1996 a separate written theory test was introduced to the Driving Test in the UK to replace questions asked about 'The Highway Code' whilst actually driving. Learner drivers were expected to know rather different information then from that published in the first edition of the Highway Code, price 1d, launched in 1931.

- In 1931 mirrors were not even mentioned.
- Drivers were advised to sound their horn when overtaking.
- At least 8 pages showed the various hand signals a driver should use. There was a single page in the current edition.
- Contained 18 pages (out of 24) of advice, compared to 135 pages in 2007.
- Included advice to drivers of horse drawn vehicles to 'rotate the whip above the head; then incline the whip to the right or left to show the direction in which the turn is to be made'.

It wasn't until the second edition of the Code that diagrams of road signs appeared, just 10 in all, plus a warning about the dangers of driving when tired or drinking and driving.

Renault Clio

Advertising for the first-generation Renault Clio introduced us to 'Nicole *et* Papa' and gave the small car a personality that appealed to drivers of all ages.

Ford Focus

The Focus replaced the previously very successful Escort. Ford wanted a 'World Car' to sell across all markets so the Focus was born and is still produced.

Toyota Previa

Toyota created the multi- purpose vehicle market with the Spacecruiser in the 80s, but the futuristic replacement, the Toyota Previa was a whole new approach to the people carrier.

Lexus LS 400

Toyota moved into the luxury market with the Lexus brand. The Lexus' flagship model is one of the most reliable vehicles ever built.

COCOTAXI

The auto-rickshaw began in Havana in the 1990s and soon spread to the whole of Cuba. These gas-scooters are named after their shape, that of a coconut and are made of a fibreglass shell with seats welded onto it. They can travel at about 30mph and because they are small, they weave and squeeze in and out of the city traffic. Blue Cocotaxis are for locals, yellow for tourists.

MOTORCYCLES

During the 1990s motorcycles started to evolve more quickly and there was a resurgence in the British biking industry with Triumph starting up production.

A bike lovers favourite however, was the 1995, Aprilia RS250.

NEW YEAR'S EVE 1999
The Millennium Bug

Whilst the world was getting 'ready to party' there was an undercurrent of anxiety about the Y2K (year 2000) Bug and many people were scared. When complicated computer programmes were first written in the 1960s, programmers used a two-digit code for the year, leaving out the "19." As the year 2000 approached, many believed that the systems would not interpret the "00" correctly, making the year 2000 indistinguishable from 1900 causing a major malfunction.

It was particularly worrying to certain organisations. Banks calculate the rate for interest owed daily and instead of the rate for one day, if the 'clocks went back' their computers would calculate a rate of interest for **minus** 100 years!

Airlines felt they were at a very great risk. All scheduled flights are recorded on computers and liable to be affected and, if the computer reverted to 1900, well, there were very few airline flights that year!
Power plants were threatened, depending on routine computer maintenance for safety checks, such as water pressure or radiation levels, the wrong date would wreck the calculations and possibly put nearby residents at risk.

Huge sums were spent to prepare for the consequences and both software and hardware companies raced to fix it by developing "Y2K compliant" programmes. Midnight passed on the 1 January 2000 and the crisis failed to materialise - planes did not fall from the sky, power stations did not melt down and thousands of people who had stocked up on food, water, even arms, or purchased backup generators or withdrawn large sums of money in anticipation of a computer-induced apocalypse, could breathe easily again.

The Millennium Dome

Officially called the O2, the huge construction and tourist attraction alongside the Thames in Greenwich, London was initially built to house an exhibition for the approach of the 21st Century. Designed by Sir Richard Rogers, the central dome is the largest in the world. On December 31, 1999, a New Year's Eve celebration at the dome was attended by some 10,500 people, including the Prime Minister, Tony Blair, and the Queen. Opening the next day, the Millennium Dome exhibition lasted until December 31, 2000.

AND A NEW MILLENNIUM

Memorabilia and Monuments

The Millennium Wheel Better known as the London Eye, at 135m (443 ft) it is Europe's tallest cantilevered observation wheel. Situated on the South Bank of the Thames when opened it used to offer the highest public viewing point in London until superseded in 2013 by the 245m high (804 ft) observation deck on the 72nd floor of The Shard.

Portsmouth's Millennium Tower opened five years late and officials were so concerned that people may actually have forgotten what the millennium was, that they gave it a new name, **The Spinnaker Tower**.

The Millennium Bridge is a steel suspension bridge for pedestrians over the River Thames linking Bankside with the City of London. Londoners nicknamed it the "Wobbly Bridge" after pedestrians experienced an alarming swaying motion on its opening day.

Lots of memorabilia was produced to mark the new millennium.
Some pieces are timeless classics and others will soon be forgotten.

2000:

Jan: Celebrations take place throughout the UK on the 1st and the Millennium Dome is officially opened by The Queen.

Aug 4th: Queen Elizabeth the Queen Mother celebrates her hundredth birthday

2001:

Feb: The Foot and Mouth disease crisis begins. Over 6 million cows and sheep are killed to halt the disease.

Jun: Labour wins the General Election. David Cameron is a new entrant, Edward Heath retires, and William Hague resigns as leader of the Conservatives.

2002:

Jan: The Euro is officially introduced in the Eurozone countries.

Jun: The Golden Jubilee. A special service is held in St Paul's Cathedral to mark the Queen's 50 years on the throne. Celebrations take place all over the country.

2003:

Mar: The United States, along with coalition forces primarily from the United Kingdom, initiates war on Iraq

May: BBC Radio 4 airs a report stating that the government claimed in its dossier, that Iraq could deploy weapons of mass destruction within forty-five minutes knowing the claim to be dubious.

Jul: Dr David Kelly, the weapons expert who was the reporter's source, is found dead.

2004:

Jan: The Hutton Inquiry into the circumstances of the death of Dr Kelly is published. The UK media, in general, condemns the report as a whitewash.

Jul: A new Countryside Code is published in advance of the 'Right to Roam' coming into effect in September across England and Wales.

TERRORISM

2001: On the 11th September, Al-Qaeda terrorists hijack civilian airliners and fly two into the Twin Towers of the World Trade Centre in New York, which collapse. There are 3,000 fatalities including 67 British nationals.

SOCIAL MEDIA

2004: In February, Mark Zuckerberg launches 'The Facebook', later renamed 'Facebook' as an online social networking website for Harvard University Students. In 2006 it was opened up to anyone over the age of 13.

21st Century

Explosion

2005: On the morning of 11 December, the UK experienced its largest explosion since World War Two. A huge blast at the Buncefield fuel depot in Hemel Hempstead, was heard as far away as the Netherlands and caused the UK's biggest blaze in peacetime which shrouded much of south-east England in smoke.

High Speed Trains

2007: In November, the Queen officially opened 'High Speed 1' and 'St Pancras International' station. The Channel Tunnel first opened to Eurostar in 1994, with trains running from Waterloo, but the new 69-mile link meant the journey from London to Paris reduced to 2 hrs 15 minutes and to Brussels 1 hr 51 min.

2005:
Apr: Prince Charles marries Camilla Parker Bowles at a private ceremony at Windsor Guildhall.

Aug: Hurricane Katrina devastates much of the U.S. Gulf Coast from Louisiana to the Florida Panhandle killing an estimated 1,836 people

2006:
Jul: Twitter is launched, becoming one of the largest social media platforms in the world.

Nov: Alexander Litvinenko a British-naturalised Russian defector dies of polonium poisoning in London.

2007:
Jun: Tony Blair resigns as Prime Minister and Gordon Brown is elected unopposed.

Jul: England introduces a ban on smoking in enclosed public places in line with Scotland, Wales and N. Ireland.

2008:
Mar: Terminal 5 is opened at London Heathrow but IT problems cause over 500 flights to be cancelled

Nov: St Hilda's College admits male undergraduates and ceases to be the last single-sex college at Oxford.

Dec: Woolworths shuts down in the UK.

2009:
Jul: The largest haul of Anglo-Saxon treasure ever found, the Staffordshire Hoard, is first uncovered buried beneath a field near Litchfield. 4,600 items amounting to 11 lb of gold, 3lb of silver and 3.5k pieces of garnet cloisonné jewellery.

Oct: The independent audit of MPs expenses is completed and exposes a widespread parliamentary scandal.

2010:

Jan: In the Chilcott Inquiry, set up in 2009, Tony Blair is questioned in public for the first time about his decision to take the UK to war against Iraq.

May: The General Election results in a Hung Parliament. An alliance is formed between the Tories and the Liberal Democrats.

2011:

Feb: An earthquake of 6.3 magnitude devastates Christchurch, New Zealand. Hundreds of people are killed.

Apr: Prince William marries Catherine Middleton in Westminster Abbey.

2012:

Jun: The UK begins celebrations of the Queen's Diamond Jubilee. Events include a pageant on the Thames and a Pop Concert outside Buckingham Palace

Jul: The summer Olympic Games are held in London, making it the first city to host them for a third time.

2013:

Jul: A new Marriage Act receives Royal Assent and same-sex marriage becomes legal in England and Wales.

Aug: A burger, grown from bovine stem cells in a laboratory, is cooked and eaten in London. The same month, a 15 ton 'fatburg' is removed after completely blocking a London sewer.

2014:

Mar: Prince Harry launches the Invictus Games for wounded soldiers.

Mar: The first gay weddings take place in England and Wales.

THE SHARD

2012: In July, The Shard, an iconic 'vertical city' is officially opened in London. It is the tallest building in Europe and the tallest habitable free-standing structure in the UK at 1,016ft (309.6 m)

THE ARAB SPRING

2010: 'The Arab Spring', a series of anti-government protests, uprisings, and armed rebellions spread across much of the Arab world. Starting in Tunisia it spread to Libya, Egypt, Yemen, Syria and Bahrain. Amongst leaders to be deposed was Gaddafi of Libya.

BREXIT

June 2016: After months of heated, angry argument and debate, the referendum on whether to leave the EU or remain within it, is held. Nearly 30m people take part and the result is to leave the EU: 51.9% votes to 48.1%.

March 2017: Article 50 is invoked and the two-year countdown to departure begins.

March 2019: Parliament rejected Theresa May's EU withdrawal agreement and a new deadline is set by The European Council to leave, with or without an Agreement, at the end of Oct 2019.

Jun 2019: Unable to 'deliver Brexit', Theresa May steps down and in Jul 2019: Boris Johnson becomes Prime Minister.

Oct 2019: The deadline to leave passes, and the EU agrees to a new date, end of Jan 2020. Commemorative Brexit coins are melted down.

Jan 2020: Johnson signs the Withdrawal Agreement.

January 31st 2020: At 11pm, the UK leaves the European Union and marks the moment with a party in Parliament Square.

2015:
Jan: Two Al-Qaeda gunmen kill 12 and injure 11 more at the Paris headquarters of the satirical newspaper Charlie Hebdo.

May: The General Election is won by David Cameron for the Conservatives with an outright majority of 331 seats.
Jun: The 800th anniversary of the Magna Carta.

2016:
Jun: The UK Referendum to leave the EU, Brexit, takes place and the majority vote is 'Yes'. David Cameron later resigns.
Jul: On July 14, Bastille Day (Independence Day), a terrorist drives a truck through a crowded promenade in Nice, France. 87 people are killed.
Nov: Donald Trump becomes US President.

2017:
There are a string of deadly terror attacks in Britain including : Westminster Bridge, the Manchester Arena and London Bridge.
Jun: The Tories lose their majority in Theresa May's general election gamble.

2018:
Apr: The UK, France, and United States order the bombing of Syrian military bases.

May: Prince Harry marries the American actress Meghan Markle in St George's Chapel, Windsor Castle. It is thought 1.9m people watched on TV worldwide.

2019:
Jun: Theresa May resigns as Prime Minister. Before she goes, she agrees a new legally binding target to reach net zero by 2050.
Jul: Boris Johnson becomes Prime Minister.

1943 Calendar

January
S	M	T	W	T	F	S
					1	2
3	4	5	6	7	8	9
10	11	12	13	14	15	16
17	18	19	20	21	22	23
24	25	26	27	28	29	30
31						

February
S	M	T	W	T	F	S
	1	2	3	4	5	6
7	8	9	10	11	12	13
14	15	16	17	18	19	20
21	22	23	24	25	26	27
28						

March
S	M	T	W	T	F	S
	1	2	3	4	5	6
7	8	9	10	11	12	13
14	15	16	17	18	19	20
21	22	23	24	25	26	27
28	29	30	31			

April
S	M	T	W	T	F	S
				1	2	3
4	5	6	7	8	9	10
11	12	13	14	15	16	17
18	19	20	21	22	23	24
25	26	27	28	29	30	

May
S	M	T	W	T	F	S
						1
2	3	4	5	6	7	8
9	10	11	12	13	14	15
16	17	18	19	20	21	22
23	24	25	26	27	28	29
30	31					

June
S	M	T	W	T	F	S
		1	2	3	4	5
6	7	8	9	10	11	12
13	14	15	16	17	18	19
20	21	22	23	24	25	26
27	28	29	30			

July
S	M	T	W	T	F	S
				1	2	3
4	5	6	7	8	9	10
11	12	13	14	15	16	17
18	19	20	21	22	23	24
25	26	27	28	29	30	31

August
S	M	T	W	T	F	S
1	2	3	4	5	6	7
8	9	10	11	12	13	14
15	16	17	18	19	20	21
22	23	24	25	26	27	28
29	30	31				

September
S	M	T	W	T	F	S
			1	2	3	4
5	6	7	8	9	10	11
12	13	14	15	16	17	18
19	20	21	22	23	24	25
26	27	28	29	30		

October
S	M	T	W	T	F	S
					1	2
3	4	5	6	7	8	9
10	11	12	13	14	15	16
17	18	19	20	21	22	23
24	25	26	27	28	29	30
31						

November
S	M	T	W	T	F	S
	1	2	3	4	5	6
7	8	9	10	11	12	13
14	15	16	17	18	19	20
21	22	23	24	25	26	27
28	29	30				

December
S	M	T	W	T	F	S
			1	2	3	4
5	6	7	8	9	10	11
12	13	14	15	16	17	18
19	20	21	22	23	24	25
26	27	28	29	30	31	

Printed in Great Britain
by Amazon

19411263R00088